AMERICAN HERITAGE

April 1967 · Volume XVIII, Number 3

HONISS OYSTER HOUSE, HARTFORD

CARELESS JONES, A PARODY FOR RAIL BUFFS

Scene: *The New York, New Haven & Hartford roundhouse at Hartford, Connecticut*
Time: *Early Saturday morning, July 8, 1905*

Enter a group of engine hostlers

1ST HOSTLER.   Come, all you roundhousemen, I want you to hear
        The story told of a dumb engineer;
    Careless Jones was the bounder's name,
        On the New York-Hartford run he rode to fame.

CHORUS.   Careless Jones—dismounted from his cabin;
        Careless Jones—left the boiler full of steam;
    Careless Jones—forgot to throw the brake in,
        And the engine almost plunged into the flowing stream.

Exeunt omnes, steaming.

AMERICAN HERITAGE

The Magazine of History

SENIOR EDITOR
Bruce Catton

EDITOR
Oliver Jensen
MANAGING EDITOR
Robert L. Reynolds
ART DIRECTOR
Murray Belsky
ASSOCIATE EDITORS
E. M. Halliday
Joan Paterson Kerr
ASSISTANT EDITORS
David G. Lowe
Suzanne A. Smith
Douglas Tunstell
CONTRIBUTING EDITORS
Mary Cable
Walter Karp
Barbara Klaw
COPY EDITOR: Brenda Niemand
EDITORIAL ASSISTANT
Mary Dawn Earley

PUBLISHER
Darby Perry

ADVISORY BOARD
Allan Nevins, *Chairman*

Carl Carmer | Louis C. Jones
Gerald Carson | Alvin M. Josephy, Jr.
Marshall B. Davidson | Howard H. Peckham
John A. Garraty | Francis S. Ronalds
Eric F. Goldman | S. K. Stevens

AMERICAN HERITAGE is published every two months by American Heritage Publishing Co., Inc., 551 Fifth Avenue, New York, N.Y. 10017.

PRESIDENT
James Parton
CHAIRMAN, EDITORIAL COMMITTEE
Joseph J. Thorndike
EDITORIAL DIRECTOR, BOOK DIVISION
Richard M. Ketchum
SENIOR ART DIRECTOR
Irwin Glusker

Correspondence about subscriptions should be sent to: American Heritage Subscription Office, 383 West Center Street, Marion, Ohio 43301. Single copies: $3.95. Annual subscriptions: $15.00 in U.S. and Canada; $16.00 elsewhere.

An annual Index of AMERICAN HERITAGE is published every February, priced at $1.00.

AMERICAN HERITAGE will consider but assumes no responsibility for unsolicited materials. Title registered U.S. Patent Office. Second-class postage paid at New York, N.Y., and at additional mailing offices.

Sponsored by

American Association for State & Local History · Society of American Historians

CONTENTS   *April, 1967 · Volume XVIII, Number 3*

COVER: It was 1910 and the motorcar was just the thing for a sport and his girl when this song was written about the new gas eater put out by the Cole people of Indianapolis. "*You will win me, Bill, heart and soul,/If you buy a Cole*" begins the somewhat crass lyric, but the song-sheet cover is handsome, and we are indebted for it to collector Lester S. Levy of Baltimore. Who could know in that joyful era that the automobile, which seemed so innocent, would cover untrodden ways with concrete cloverleafs, destroy the railroads, and poison the air of our cities? Gerald Carson, our walking delegate to Old Nostalgia, writes entertainingly of these early days, beginning on page 32. *Back Cover*: This sign hung for many years at Bissell's Tavern, operated at South Windsor, Connecticut, by the family who had run the Connecticut River ferry there ever since 1648. Now the sign is no longer an ad but an artifact (a step up or down, depending on your point of view), and hangs at the Connecticut Historical Society. Times do change. Yankee children from Rhode Island and Boston no longer think that the long and beautiful Connecticut marks the beginning of the American West. On its history and durable charms, Ellsworth Grant of Hartford writes an affectionate essay beginning on page 46.

The Grimké sisters forsook their heritage to fight for abolition. Then,

The Grimkés lived on Charleston's Battery; this view was painted in 1831, shortly after Sarah and Angelina left. They were never

A FAMILY DIVIDED

By JANET STEVENSON

reconciled with their patrician parents, Mary and John (below).

It was 1868, five years after the Emancipation Proclamation, three years after the end of the war that made it stick and the death of the President who wrote it.

Most of the old prewar abolitionist periodicals had ceased to publish. A few—among them the *Anti-Slavery Standard*—still circulated among a select list of old subscribers which included Sarah Grimké and her sister Angelina Grimké Weld, whose famous eyewitness account of American slavery had shaken the pillars of the southern Establishment and roused the northern conscience thirty years before.

In the January issue of the *Standard*, Angelina saw an article signed by a Professor Bowers of Lincoln University in Oxford, Pennsylvania, an institution devoted to the higher education of Negro youth. The article reported in enthusiastic terms an oration delivered "by a young man but a few years removed from the chains of servitude, whose erudition and felicity of expression would be remarkable in any student in any college..." The name of the young man was Archibald Henry Grimké.

Angelina had never heard of him, and neither had Sarah. Both were made profoundly uneasy by the coincidence of the name, and—characteristically—Angelina decided to take direct action. On February 15, 1868, she wrote to the young man:

In a recent number of the *Anti-Slavery Standard* I saw a notice of a meeting at Lincoln University of a Literary Society at which a young gentleman of the name of Grimké deliver'd an address. My maiden name was Grimké. I am the youngest sister of Dr. John Grimké of So. Carolina, & as this name is a very uncommon one it has occurred to me that you had been probably the slave of one of my brothers & I feel a great desire to know all about you.

My Sister Sarah & myself have long been interested in the Anti-Slavery cause, & left Charleston nearly 40 years ago, because we could not endure to live in the midst of the oppressions of Slavery. Will you therefore be so kind as to tell us who you are, whether you have any brothers & sisters —who your parents were etc. etc. . . .

Angelina showed her letter to her husband and to Sarah, but she did not ask their consent to the sending of it. All three knew what alternative answers to her questions were possible, and what Angelina stood to lose if the worst of those possibilities materialized. She was jeopardizing her physical and mental health— if not her life—by the inquiry. But no one in that household would have dreamed of trying to dissuade Angelina from any course of action she had determined was right.

Angelina was at the time sixty-three years old, a frail, gray gentlewoman with a soft southern voice who taught English and history at Dr. Dio Lewis' boarding school for young ladies in Lexington, Massachusetts. Mr. Weld also taught at the school. Vigorous and keen even at sixty-five, he enjoyed the fame of having once been the most effective abolitionist orator in the country. It was almost forgotten—and quite hard to believe—that his wife had been equally effective and even more famous (or infamous) in her day. Wendell Phillips, who had been considered the great orator of abolitionism, said of Angelina, "She swept the cords of the human heart with a power that has never been surpassed and rarely equalled. . . . She won Massachusetts for abolition—and it was never lost again."

But all that was far in the past. Since the evening—just two days after her marriage—when she spoke in Pennsylvania Hall in Philadelphia and outfaced the mob that had come to burn it, Angelina had neither addressed nor attended a public meeting. It was accepted by those who knew her history that she had "shattered her nervous system" and worn out her physical strength in the service of abolition, and that the bearing of three children had completed the wreck. She lived a "half life," a long anticlimax to her brief apocalyptic career, avoiding every sort of strain or excitement at the peril of a "nervous prostration" that would put her to bed in a darkened room for weeks at a time. She had earned the right to—if not a taste for—peace.

Angelina was born in 1805, the youngest daughter of a well-to-do Charleston judge. She was in her early twenties, following the conventional course of a young lady of quality, when the preaching of a Presbyterian evangelist awoke in her a desire for a deeper commitment to the spiritual life. She left her family's fashionable Episcopalian church and began to seek salvation through good works—in the main, through efforts to alleviate the suffering of Negro slaves. In this she was probably guided by the example of her elder sister Sarah who had already turned against slavery and gone north to join the Society of Friends.

But if Angelina began by following in the footsteps of Sarah (who was twelve years older, and whom she called her "sister-mother"), she soon caught up with and passed her. During the most important years of their adult lives—from about 1830 to 1838—it was Angelina who led and Sarah who followed—on a path that led straight into the heart of the storm.

Left: Slave auctions were among the horrors that impelled the sensitive Grimké sisters toward abolitionism. Years later, in an exchange of letters (right), they learned they had Negro nephews whose own white half brother had abused them.

Angelina Grimké   *Sarah Grimké*

"Mr. Grimké, Dear Sir:
. . . I am the youngest sister of Dr. John Grimké of So. Carolina, & as this name is a very uncommon one . . . will you . . . tell us who you are?"

"Dear Madam:
. . . I am the son of Henry Grimké, a brother of Dr. John Grimké . . .
Mr. E. M. Grimké (Henry's son) . . . wanted a boy to wait on him. He informed my mother that she should send me to his house. . . . I afterwards fled from my oppressor. Frank attempted to escape but was retaken & sold . . ."

Archibald (left) and Francis Grimké

Even before 1829, when Angelina went to Philadelphia to join Sarah in her meeting, she had become a Quaker in her own mind. She had sought out and been accepted by the only two Quakers in Charleston —two old men who met for silent worship every Sunday "in a dingy little meetinghouse on the outskirts of the city." She had adopted the gray garb and the plain speech of the Quakers, because she felt that to do so in Charleston would indicate a protest against slavery. But the going had been hard and the results disappointing. She expected to find in the city of William Penn a richer spiritual companionship and a higher level of ethical behavior, especially on the question of slavery. "What was her amazement to find that the Religious Society of Friends, whose moral courage in rebuke of slavery had put to shame all other churches—that *they* had installed the 'Negro pew' as a permanent fixture in their house of worship!"*

Sarah had silently endured this painful contradiction between the Friends' "witness" and their practice for the several years she had lived among them. But Angelina encouraged her to rebel. "Whenever, in city or country, they entered a church having a Negro seat (then they *all* had), they found their way to it," Weld later wrote of the sisters, "and shared with the occupants the spurning thus meted out to them."

What distressed Angelina even more was the ban on all discussion of the subject with the meeting. Slavery had become so controversial that it threatened the unity of the group, which most Friends felt had to be preserved at any cost. But she did her best to abide by the ban and other accepted rules of conduct while she undertook a course of study and meditation designed to prepare her for a "ministry" (in the Quaker sense of that term). She was advised to turn her mind inward and to seek the "peace that passeth understanding."

But the times were not propitious for such peace. In 1829, in the same month that Angelina came to Philadelphia, William Lloyd Garrison published the first issue of the *Liberator,* with its bold declaration that "I will be as harsh as truth, and as uncompromising as justice...I will not equivocate—I will not excuse—I will not retreat a single inch—AND I WILL BE HEARD."

Angelina may have been one of his first subscribers. At any rate, she was a regular reader by 1835, when, as Wendell Phillips said, "our cities roared with riot, when William Lloyd Garrison was dragged through

TEXT CONTINUED ON PAGE 84

* These and many other passages quoted here referring to Angelina's history are taken from a sketch written by her husband after her death, and privately published by George E. Ellis of Boston, under the title *In Memory*. The passages quoting Wendell Phillips and Elizur Wright are taken from the same source.

8

THE GREAT CRUSADE: 1830–63

Before the year 1830, when Theodore Weld began preaching the gospel of abolitionism—a crusade in which the Grimké sisters would soon join him—hardly a single noted American advocated the prompt abolition of slavery within the United States. It was not that the slave system had many ardent defenders, but that it had few ardent enemies. Conscientious men expected it to die out naturally, while the majority of Americans hardly thought about it at all. The South's "peculiar institution," it was felt, was no one's concern but the South's. A few years later, a quarter of a million Americans, organized in two thousand chapters of the American Anti-Slavery Society, had come to believe that slavery was a sin, a crime, an abomination so loathsome that nothing but its immediate extirpation could save the nation's soul. This was the achievement of the abolitionists, a small, fervent band of men and women incredibly brave, righteous to a fault, and disliked by most of their countrymen. At first they were jeered at and beaten. They were despised for offering no plan or program for the enormous task of emancipation. But they were indifferent to plans; they had only one aim: to force Americans to look upon the face of slavery— upon the mute misery of such as the woman shown opposite—and repent. The most eloquent and tireless agitators America had ever seen, the abolitionists made themselves heard, even by the politicians and men of power. As the cause became more and more a northern cause, the two halves of the nation drew tragically apart. They little knew, these abolition zealots, what forces they had set in motion by their simple evangelical appeal, or how long and bloody the road to full emancipation would be. Some of the major mileposts—and pilgrims—along that road are described on the next seventeen pages.

PICTURE CREDITS FOR PORTFOLIO ON PAGE 88

A RACE
IN BONDAGE

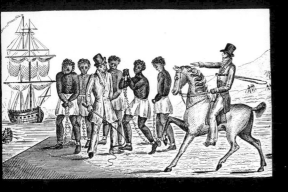

After the Sale; Slaves Going South, painted by a visiting Englishman, Eyre Crowe, in 1853

American slavery was a degrading system. In other times and places, bondsmen could acquire wealth, maintain a family, even buy their freedom. In America, however, they were just property: raping a neighbor's female slave, for example, was considered merely as trespassing. And the slave was property that multiplied itself. The one million slaves in 1808 (when Congress prohibited further importation) grew to almost four million by 1860. Prices rose steadily too, and commerce in human beings became a thriving enterprise for jobbers who bought blacks in Virginia and drove them like cattle to the auctions in New Orleans. By 1830 it was clear that slavery, far from becoming extinct, was more deeply entrenched than ever

A FLAME IS LIGHTED

The abolition movement, in its beginnings, was a religious crusade with strong roots in Ohio. There a group of seminarians, including a Connecticut-born *Mayflower* descendant named Henry Stanton, had come to believe that the godly must work for human betterment. Their leader was the brilliant Weld, a young reformer whom people likened to an archangel. A compelling figure who had already converted a southern lawyer named James G. Birney to his lifelong struggle for Negro freedom, Weld convinced his fellow students to take up abolition as *the* Christian cause. Moving in a body to tiny Oberlin College (above) near Cleveland, they helped turn it into a great reform center and from it went out into the countryside calling upon men of conscience to join in purging the sin of slavery from the land.

Theodore Weld

Henry Stanton

James G. Birney

At first, the abolitionists aroused ferocious antagonism. In November of 1837 a mob set fire to a warehouse in Alton, Illinois (below), where the abolitionist editor Elijah P. Lovejoy had stored his printing press; Lovejoy was shot dead. That winter in Philadelphia, antislavery adherents built Pennsylvania Hall (above) as a haven for free speech. Its first speaker was Angelina Grimké, and she barely escaped with her life. The next day, the mobs returned and demolished the building. For abolitionists, these early years were an age of martyrs.

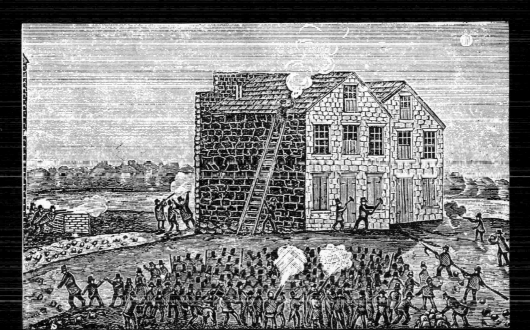

Lucretia Mott

Prudence Crandall

THE GOSPEL SPREADS

John Quincy Adams

William Slade

ment itself more complex than in the evangelistic West. Abolitionists could list among their unflinching supporters the Boston patrician Wendell Phillips (seen opposite in a painting by Alexander Rosenfeldt), who first spoke out when he heard a lecturer liken the murderers of Lovejoy to the patriots who dumped tea into Boston Harbor. Phillips attacked the lecturer: "For the sentiments he has uttered, on soil consecrated by the prayers of Puritans and the blood of patriots, the earth should have yawned and swallowed him up." Almost alone among militant abolitionists, the eloquent Phillips held the admiration of men who disliked the cause he stood for.

Strong in the eastern movement were women—ranging from Lucretia Mott, the Quaker founder of the Philadelphia Female Anti-Slavery League, to a stubborn young teacher named Prudence Crandall, who created a national furor by daring to teach Negro girls at her private boarding school in Connecticut. To stop her the state legislature passed a law making the teaching of integrated classes a crime. The law's dubious constitutionality helped draw together radical abolitionists and more reputable guardians of constitutional liberty, a key step in winning adherents to the cause. In fact, it was by exploiting the constitutional issue that aged ex-President John Quincy Adams became antislavery's first great champion in Congress. The stand he took was not, at first, against slavery, but against a House rule that automatically tabled any petition relating to slavery. Alone in the House except for a few supporters like William Slade of Vermont, Adams defied the fury of the entire chamber and introduced one antislavery petition after another. When at last in 1844 he succeeded in defeating the rule, the taboo against discussing slavery in Congress was destroyed forever. The abolitionist movement had now entered national politics.

ABOLITIONISM'S FAR LEFT

William Lloyd Garrison

To denounce slavery was one thing, to do something about it was a knottier matter—except among the extremists. Few families were more conspicuously antislavery than the Beechers (below), gifted children of the great preacher Lyman Beecher. Yet even they had their doubts. Did the federal government possess the power—Henry Ward Beecher asked—to abolish slavery in the states? Was the crusade, as Harriet Beecher Stowe's sister Catharine believed, doing more harm than good? No such doubts troubled William Lloyd Garrison, editor of the abolition journal the *Liberator*. He called slaveowners "thieves" and the Constitution a "covenant with hell." Garrison was a pacifist, but John Brown (opposite), a Garrisonian with "a little touch of insanity about his glittering gray-blue eyes," was not. At Harpers Ferry, Virginia, in 1859, as the self-styled instrument of Providence, Brown set in motion his plan to end slavery by force—and was hanged. But his spirit went marching on.

Thomas	William	Edward		Charles	Henry Ward
Isabella	Catharine	Dr. Lyman Beecher	Mary	Harriet	

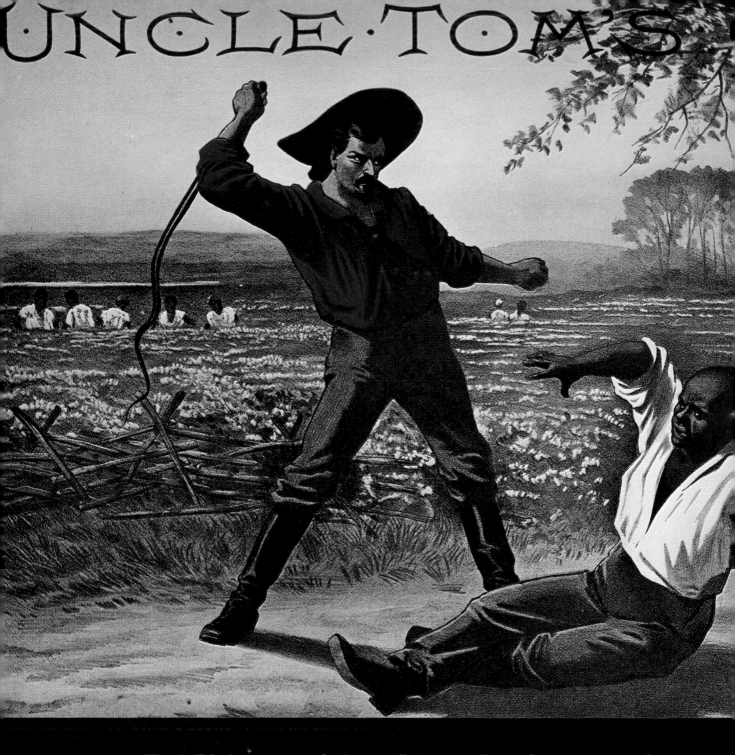

The abolitionists were amazingly versatile propagandists, using every means of communication available in a largely rural society. Antislavery lectures, like the one announced at far right above, often featured the latest victim of the "Slave Power"; they had the fervor of revival meetings. Antislavery ideals and pictures were broadcast in the durable form of almanacs, while New York's John Rogers sculpted poignant antislavery scenes and cast them in plaster for mass distribution. But nothing compared to the explosion created in 1852 by Mrs. Stowe's *Uncle Tom's Cabin*, the most immediately popular book ever written. Within one year, some 300,000 Americans bought copies, and thousands saw stage adaptations like the one advertised above. Any good "Tom show" made a great scene out of Simon Legree whipping the poor black hero, whose saintly forbearance under extreme provocation turned his name into a derogatory epithet

VOL. I. NO. 5.

THE
AMERICAN
ANTI-SLAVERY
ALMANAC,
FOR
1840,

BEING BISSEXTILE OR LEAP-YEAR, AND THE 64TH OF AMERICAN INDEPENDENCE. CALCULATED FOR NEW YORK; ADAPTED TO THE NORTHERN AND MIDDLE STATES.

NORTHERN HOSPITALITY—NEW YORK NINE MONTHS' LAW.
The slave steps out of the slave state, and his chains fall. A free state, with another chain, stands ready to re-enslave him.

Thus saith the Lord, Deliver him that is spoiled out of the hands of the oppressor.

NEW YORK:
PUBLISHED BY THE AMERICAN ANTI-SLAVERY SOCIETY,
NO. 143 NASSAU STREET.

LET THE NORTH AWAKE!

T. B. M'CORMICK

Will Discuss the Immorality, Illegality and Unconstitutionality of

AMERICAN SLAVERY,

And the Duty and Power of the General Government to Abolish it.

IN

AT

Mr. M'CORMICK is the Clergyman for whom the Governor of Kentucky made a Requisition upon the Governor of Indiana, charging him with aiding in the escape of Fugitive Slaves. The Warrant was issued and Mr. M'Cormick is thereby exiled from his home. All are respectfully invited to attend.

THE FUGITIVE'S STORY
JOHN G. WHITTIER   H. W. BEECHER   W. LLOYD GARRISON

THE PROPAGANDA
OF
ANTISLAVERY

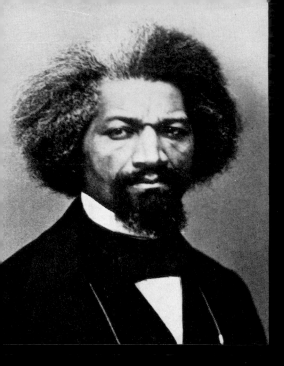

THE NEGRO
HELPS HIMSELF

The Negro, slavery's defenders claimed, was happiest as a slave, but every year thousands of bondsmen voted for freedom with their feet. The picture at right, *Slaves Escaping Through the Swamp*, was painted in 1862 by Thomas Moran; it may exaggerate the foliage, but not the perils the runaways faced, nor the desperation that gripped them. Not surprisingly, those who made good their escape to the North provided strong support for the abolitionist crusade, for as long as slavery endured, the chance of being snatched back into bondage was a very real terror. The greatest of these slaves-turned-abolitionists was Frederick Douglass (above), who had himself fled from his master in 1838. In 1841 he spoke out courageously before an antislavery convention in Nantucket, describing in a simple, faltering way his life as a slave. By 1845, when he retold it in his famed *Narrative of the Life of Frederick Douglass*, he no longer spoke haltingly. Few among the leaders of the movement were as effective in bringing the Negro's case before the American people

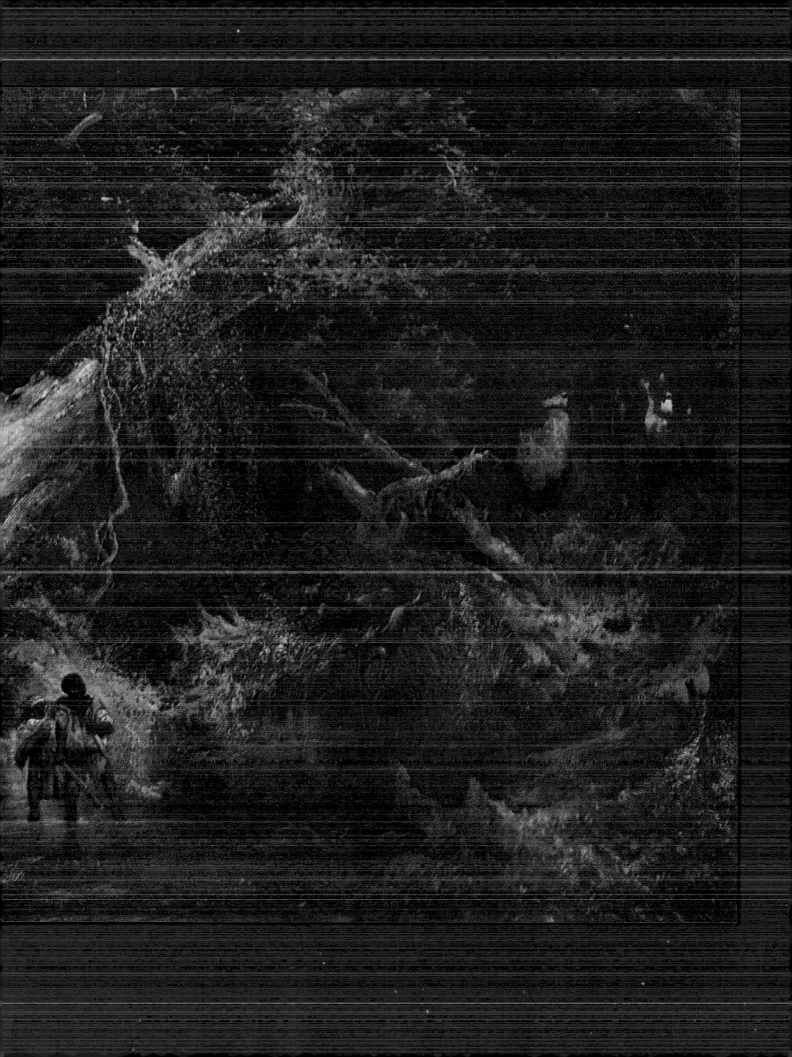

NORTH
TO
FREEDOM

It was called "the business of Egypt" or, most often, the Underground Railroad. It was a conspiracy, in fact, of otherwise law-abiding citizens to break the law by helping slaves escape, and by the 1840's the work was superbly organized. Ohio, with twenty-three ports along the river that divided slave-holding territory from free, was the great trunk route to freedom. Under cover of darkness, as Ohio artist Charles T. Webber depicted it (right), "conductors" brought fugitives to a farmhouse "station" to be fed and sheltered, then sent on to the next stop. The risks were enormous, most of all for Negro "guides" like Harriet Tubman, who slipped into the South to persuade slaves to flee and then directed their flight. During the 1850's some 75,000 men, women, and children escaped via the Underground Railroad. To southerners it was systematic theft; to many northerners it was obedience to a "higher law." Between the two sections, barely a shred of common ground was now left on the slavery controversy.

FREEDOM TO THE SLAVES.

Proclaimed January 1st 1863, by ABRAHAM LINCOLN, President of the United States.

"PROCLAIM LIBERTY THROUGHOUT ALL THE LAND UNTO ALL THE INHABITANTS THEREOF." Lev. XXV. 10.

PUBLISHED BY CURRIER & IVES   115 NASSAU ST. NEW YORK

A LONG,
LONG WAY
TO GO

1863: The unchaining, shown
in a Currier & Ives print
1966: James Meredith, shot in
Mississippi while encouraging Negro voters to register

THE PASSION OF HERNANDO DE SOTO

In Florida the great conquistador hoped to find

a Golconda. Instead, he found a Golgotha

By TIMOTHY SEVERIN

Before the days of the explorers, the Mississippi was an Indian river. Spreading in a vast belt from the Great Lakes to the Gulf of Mexico was a multitude of tribes—Fox, Potawatomi, Kickapoo, Iowa, Illinois, Winnebago, Miami, Masouten, Chickasaw, Oto, Quapaw, and others. These Indians were in a constant state of turmoil, fighting one another and moving up and down the river. Even the Sioux, now 'associated with the Great Plains, were once a river tribe and paddled fleets of war canoes on the upper Mississippi. The aborigines used a variety of names to describe the river, but it was the Algonquian name, "Mississippi," which finally won out. French traders heard it from the Chippewa and the other northern tribes and carried it downstream with them, until this word, variously translated as "Big Water" or "Father of Waters," became the accepted name from Montreal to Louisiana.

The fact that the Indians were often friendly and peaceable toward the white man, and that there were no difficult cataracts or rapids for most of the river's course, made the Mississippi easy to explore. Despite this there was a gap of three centuries between the date when white men first saw the river and the time of the final discovery of its source, small lakes in upper Minnesota, about 175 miles from the Canadian border. One reason for this lag is the nature of the Mississippi delta, which is awkward to find from the sea and dangerous to navigate. Only when the Spaniards probed inland did they find the continent's largest river.

In the north, climate was a great obstacle. French explorers, approaching the river from their colonies on the St. Lawrence, had to face winters in which temperatures of thirty degrees below zero were not uncommon, the land was covered with deep snow, and the river was icebound. The rigorous winters limited travelling time, increased costs, and deterred all but the brave or the ignorant from winter journeys. In summer, however, the French had an advantage over the Spanish explorers of the lower Mississippi: the birchbark canoe. This lightweight, tough, maneuverable vessel was known only to the northern tribes for the very good reason that the paper birch (*Betula papyrifera*) from which it is made grows no farther south than Wisconsin.

But the most important reasons for the delay in exploring the Mississippi were political. The river was controlled at various periods by the Spanish, French, British, and Americans. Each nation was usually more concerned with protecting its sovereignty than with exploring the stream to its source. The first major French expedition turned back when it was halfway down the river because of fear of the Spaniards. Neither the Spanish, the French, nor the British held the Mississippi long enough to invest in costly expeditions of discovery. The Americans, the eventual owners, were the first to spend substantial amounts of money on pure exploration.

As if international rivalries were not enough, many of the explorers were embroiled in quarrels with their

Hernando de Soto's discovery of the Mississippi on May 8, 1511, was romanticized three centuries later by William Henry Powell for the rotunda of the Capitol in Washington. Actually the Spanish, including their chaplains, were in rags; they had no artillery; their tools and weapons were patched-up makeshifts, for they had lost most of their baggage in a fight with the Choctaw near present-day Mobile, and what was left had been nearly destroyed when Chickasaw burned their camp.

own countrymen. The French, the most successful travellers along the river, were the worst culprits in this respect. Their explorers were constantly hampered by lawsuits of one sort or another, usually brought against them by vindictive rivals who were jealous of any commercial advantage that might accrue to the successful pioneer.

The early exploration of the Father of Waters, unlike that of the Nile or the Niger, was not carried out under the aegis of geographical societies or learned committees, but, for the greater part, by private persons who anticipated some sort of gain for themselves —gold, furs, or glory. In consequence, the river's exploration took place in fits and starts, depending upon the activities of these opportunists. Otherwise, the river was little used, because, in the words of Mark Twain, "nobody happened to want such a river;

nobody needed it, nobody was curious about it; so . . . the Mississippi remained out of the market and undisturbed. When de Soto found it, he was not hunting for a river, and had no present occasion for one; consequently he did not value it or even take any particular notice of it."

Hernando de Soto was probably the first discoverer of the river, although earlier explorers under the banner of Spain undoubtedly approached it. In 1497, Amerigo Vespucci is believed to have entered the Gulf of Mexico. Then, in 1519, a fleet under one Alonso Alvarez de Piñeda searched along the Gulf coast for the mythical sea route to the Indies. In the course of this voyage he entered the mouth of a river which he said was "very large and very full." But from his descriptions of the area, which disagree with all later Spanish reports of the Mississippi delta, it would

27

appear that he sailed into Mobile Bay. Spanish cartographers called this coast Amichel, and declared it to be "too far from the Tropics" to contain gold. It was nine years before another Spaniard, Pánfilo de Narváez, explored the coast. Narváez and nearly all his men were lost, but a few shipwrecked survivors told of a huge fresh-water current that had pushed their boat out to sea as they sailed westward; the current had been too strong for them to investigate closer inshore. But the interest of the Spanish authorities was aroused, not so much by the big river as by the survivors' report that there was gold in the interior of North America. The time had come for a full-scale invasion of Amichel by a competent commander; the man who led this invasion and who was the first to confirm the existence of the Mississippi was Hernando de Soto.

Hernando de Soto was one of the most successful men of his day and also one of its worst failures. He has been awarded a niche in American history as the first white man to set eyes on the Mississippi, but at the time he saw the river he had no idea of the importance of his discovery. The course of his extraordinary career, from humble beginnings to a life of luxury, then to a lonely, broken-hearted death on the banks of the river he discovered, unfolds like the plot in a Spanish book of chivalry.

When de Soto set out on the ill-fated Florida expedition, he was in his late thirties. He had served with Pizarro in Peru, bringing back enough booty to make him one of the richest men in Spain. But he sought power, and that meant he wanted the ultimate crown of glory for the conquistador—an independent government for himself somewhere in the New World. After marrying a rich wife with good connections, he applied for the governorship of virgin territory in what is now Ecuador and Colombia. But the King had other plans for this region and made him the counteroffer of the governorship of "Florida," the geographically vague term for the little known and as yet unconquered lands in North America bordering the Gulf of Mexico. De Soto accepted, and a formal agreement between him and the King was drawn up on April 20, 1537.

The terms of the charter were precise: de Soto was obliged to furnish at least five hundred men, and to equip and supply them for a minimum of eighteen months; the Spanish government specifically absolved itself from any financial responsibility in the venture. As his reward, de Soto was immediately made governor of Cuba, which was to be the base for his conquest of North America, and once he had conquered Florida he would also become governor, captain general, and

adelantado of any two hundred leagues of the coast he might care to select. If successful, he would receive a lifetime annuity of two thousand ducats; and this, of course, was to be paid out of income from the colony, so that the King did not have to reach into his own pocket. In return the governor of Florida promised to support any priests the Crown sent out to him. In short, he would meet every expense of the adventure and make no financial claim on the court of Spain. He would "conquer and populate," and the settlers would not have to pay taxes for the first ten years.

In exchange for the royal license, the King's treasury would receive one fifth of all gold, other precious minerals, and gems which the expedition plundered, bartered, or mined, and one half of all buried treasure. Finally, if de Soto deliberately failed to comply with any of the conditions in his license, he would be punished under the charge of high treason. The Crown could not go wrong. If de Soto was successful, the King would gain a new colony, new subjects, and a fresh supply of bullion for the royal coffers. If de Soto failed, the court would merely sympathize with his widow, comment on the sad loss of so brave and loyal a subject, and promptly issue the Florida license to somebody else.

De Soto, in fact, was not the first to hold it. Pánfilo de Narváez, Juan Ponce de León, and Lucas Vázquez de Ayllon had all tried their hand in Florida, and all had failed. But this did not stop the ambitious de Soto. First there had been great riches discovered in Mexico, then in Peru to the south; now surely, somewhere in the heart of the unknown North America a bold conquistador would find immense wealth. De Soto must certainly have heard some firm news of a Golconda, perhaps from Cabeza de Vaca, treasurer of Narváez's unsuccessful venture, who had returned from the interior tantalizingly close-mouthed about his experiences (see "The Ordeal of Cabeza de Vaca" in the December, 1960, AMERICAN HERITAGE). It was reported that but for a squabble over his contract, Cabeza de Vaca would have joined up with de Soto; as it was, he advised several of his cousins to go along on the new venture. This combination of rumor, experience, optimism, and the spirit of adventure conjured up a giant mirage of certain success. Hidalgo and peasant flocked to de Soto's recruiting officers.

Eventually 622 volunteers joined him. Among them were experienced Spanish soldiers, artisans, and priests, as well as such varied foreigners as a Greek engineer, two Genoese, four "dark men" from Africa, and even an English longbowman. The army of Florida was the youngest, the best equipped, and the most professional ever to sail from Spain to "conquer and populate" lands in the New World.

In seven vessels they put to sea on Sunday morning, April 7, 1538, joining a fleet of twenty sail bound for Mexico. The transatlantic voyage was a gay holiday. The weather held clear and the fleet stayed close together; captains and hidalgos were able to pay courtesy calls from one vessel to another and give graceful luncheons and dinners. They reached Cuba by early June, and de Soto spent a year there, establishing his governorship and planning the expedition. He had scoured Spain for supplies, sparing no expense, and now he scoured Cuba in the same manner. He even took aboard a herd of swine, a stroke of genius that gave the army a mobile larder all the way to the Mississippi and beyond. Finally he said good-bye to his wife. She did not see her husband again.

On May 30, 1539, the army began going ashore at Tampa Bay on the Florida coast. There was no sign of Indians, and the venture still had the air of a holiday. The young cavaliers were enchanted by the beauty of the scene—the dazzling blue of sea and sky, the white curve of the sand leading up to the woods of cypress, live oak, and ash. Tents and pennons rippled in the breeze, horses were exercised on the beach to shake off the effects of the voyage. The first patrols, probing inland, also succumbed to the festive mood. Small groups of lancers rode off, the sand spurting beneath the hoofs of the chargers, to hunt in the woods for Indians or deer; it did not matter which.

Soon columns of smoke rising up over the dense green of the forest showed that contact had been made with the Indians and that the natives were passing the alert from village to village. Then a patrol returned to report that the beautiful woodland was in fact hopeless country for cavalry maneuvers. The forest was a maze of ponds and marshes, separated by impassable undergrowth. The horses became entangled in thickets, or sank up to their haunches in quagmires, cutting their legs on hidden snags. Luckily, there were occasional Indian trails which followed dry ground, and on these footpaths the cavalry could improve its pace. But the trails were too narrow for more than two lancers to ride abreast, and this crippled their effectiveness; the massed charge, the favorite conquistador attack, would be out of the question in Florida. And that was not all. The patrol had surprised a small party of natives. Two of the Indians had been spitted on lances, but the others had fled into the woods, whence they began shooting arrows at their attackers from the shelter of the trees. By the time the patrol regained the safety of the open beach, two horses had been killed and several wounded. This was serious, for horses were irreplaceable and the Spanish depended on their cavalry to outmaneuver and frighten the natives. The optimistic conquistadors did not know it then, but the next four years would provide an almost daily repetition of this rough punishment, as ambush followed ambush and the invading army was raked from end to end by the stinging hit-and-run attacks of the Indians. Half the carefree cavaliers would leave their bones to whiten in *Tierra Florida,* "the land of flowers."

Not long after the landing, de Soto had a tremendous stroke of luck, possibly the only one of the whole Florida expedition. An advance patrol of cavalry came across a band of Indians in a clearing. Without pausing to consider why the Indians were exposing themselves in the open, the horsemen levelled their lances and charged. The Indians fled into the trees, leaving one man wounded on the ground and another standing there apparently in a state of shock. A trooper was just poised to run the savage through when the Indian fell to his knees, made the sign of the cross, and with difficulty cried out in halting Spanish *"Sevilla! Sevilla!"* The effect of his words was electrifying. The lancers dropped their weapons and clustered round the naked man, who explained that he was Juan Ortiz, a native of Seville who had come to Florida with Narváez's expedition, had been captured by the Indians, and had survived by going native. He had been on his way to the Spanish camp with a party of friendly Indians when the lancers had attacked them.

Juan Ortiz was a godsend for de Soto—a reliable, intelligent guide who spoke the local dialect fluently, knew the Indian customs, and could provide information on the politics and geography of the land. Ortiz was at once appointed to de Soto's staff, fed, and given communion by the priests. Uncomfortable in the close-fitting Spanish clothes after eleven years of nakedness, he went around camp dressed in a long, loose linen wrap.

The army now marched forward with more confidence. Through Ortiz, de Soto managed to establish contact with Mucozo, the friendly Indian chief who had looked after the marooned Spaniard. A peace treaty was arranged, and the Indians agreed to supply the invaders with maize and guides. But Mucozo did not possess any gold, and before long the Spaniards wore his hospitality thin. He realized that the sooner the Spanish army left, the better it would be for him and his tribe. He therefore employed a simple ruse which de Soto was to encounter again and again: he informed the Spanish general that although he himself did not have any gold, another tribe some distance away possessed legendary stores of bullion and gems. Naturally, it would take several weeks' marching to reach this glittering prize, but he, Mucozo, would gladly provide guides for the first part of the journey. These guides could lead de Soto to the limits of their tribal territory and then hand him on to Indians of the neighboring tribe.

It was a childishly naïve stratagem, but it always worked. One chief after another used the same trick to rid himself of the Spanish army, preferably diverting the unwelcome invaders into the lands of a tribal enemy. Of course, de Soto knew exactly what the Indian chiefs were plotting. Yet he had no choice but to move on. He could not afford to exhaust his men in fruitless holding operations, and he was equally worried by shortages of food. Any tribal economy could support his invading army for a limited time only. As soon as the local stocks of maize were eaten, the Spanish were compelled to move on. They assembled a marching supply of food, packed up their belongings, and forced the local cacique, or chief, to provide a small army of porters. Then the expedition snaked off through the woods, a long file of cavalry, halberdiers, crossbowmen, arquebusiers, retainers, camp followers (including one or two white women), natives, porters, and livestock. The expedition—an enormous questing centipede, groping forward, feeling a path around obstacles—headed up the Florida peninsula, thence toward what is now the state of Georgia.

The cavalry was always busy. Besides scouting ahead the lancers galloped up and down the long line of march, trying to control the unwieldy mass of porters and footmen. The horsemen had to be everywhere at once. They provided the mobile reserve in case of attack; they acted as couriers, carrying messages between the various captains; and they were allotted the undignified role of swineherds. The pigs thrived, and there were now more than three hundred of them, happily grubbing for roots and nuts on the forest floor. De Soto refused to allow his soldiers to eat the pigs. They were to be preserved against hard times, and the cursing troopers were ordered to chevy the grunting herd along the line of march, taking care not to lose a single animal.

Most of the heavy labor and transport was handled by the press-ganged Indian porters, and a steady trickle of fugitives vanished into the bush each night. As the army moved forward, however, the Spaniards noticed that they had less and less trouble from their slave labor; it was evident that once a captive Indian was outside his tribal territory he was reluctant to escape, preferring to stay with the Spanish army rather than run the risk of falling into the hands of a hostile tribe, or of being recaptured by the Spaniards, who might then throw him to their packs of vicious war dogs.

These Indians were unlike any enemy that the conquistadors had met in the New World. In Mexico and South America, campaigns had always culminated in a major battle. The native armies, no matter how vast, would be thrown into confusion by the Spaniards' horses—completely unknown to the aborigines and often believed to be flesh-eating monsters. A shrewd cavalry charge delivered with tremendous punch could turn this confusion into utter panic. But the Florida Indians would neither be forced into an open fight nor conclude a lasting peace treaty. And the Spaniards never quite grasped the extent of their bravery and tribal loyalty. One guide after another coolly led the army into swamps or ambushes, even though it was suicide for the man concerned. Even the smallest tribes put up a fight. They burned their crops and villages in a scorched-earth policy, cut off and killed isolated Spanish dispatch riders, set ambushes, and hid their food supplies from the invaders. Any solitary Spaniard wandering too near the trees was liable to get an arrow in his back, and at night the bushes around the bivouac rustled with hidden snipers. In the morning it was not uncommon to find the headless body of a Spanish soldier dangling from a tree in full view of the camp.

The steel-clad might of the Spanish veterans had run into the one obstacle it could not crush—guerrilla warfare conducted by skilled archers. The Indians used a stiff bow that discharged arrows with terrific force and considerable accuracy. In one experiment, de Soto watched a warrior put an arrow clean through a plate of Milan steel hung up in a tree eighty feet away. When a second plate was put up behind the first, the Indian put his next arrow through both pieces of armor. It was not surprising that after a skirmish the Spanish dead were sometimes found transfixed from front to back by a three-foot arrow tipped with bone, flint, or the needle-sharp claw of a crab. The most deadly arrow of all was a sharpened shaft of cane, its tip hardened over a fire. When one of these scored a direct hit on chain mail, the first six inches shattered into splinters that penetrated the interstices of the mail and left an ugly, festering wound that healed far more slowly than any sword cut. To protect themselves against these projectiles, the Spanish adopted the native armor of loose quilted jackets stuffed with cotton padding.

Even worse than the Indians were the swamps, marshes, and rivers. They delayed and exhausted the army, which often spent whole days wading chest-deep through water. Fortunately, one of the Genoese volunteers and two Cuban half-breeds were engineers and knew how to make bridges and causeways. With ropes brought specially for the purpose, they lashed logs

The somber Midnight Mass on the Mississippi Over the Body of Ferdinand de Soto, 1542 *was painted c. 1898 by Edward Moran. The obsequies were probably even more furtive: his men did not want the Indians to know the demigod was dead.*

together to make roads across the worst obstacles. At the shallower rivers the horsemen would ride their mounts into the stream and form a long line from bank to bank. Then the footmen would scramble across, clinging to stirrups, girth bands, and manes. Once or twice crude rafts were improvised, or a block-and-tackle arrangement was used to reel the less willing animals in to the opposite bank.

As the Spaniards pushed northward, de Soto found himself more and more isolated. His line of communication with Tampa became too tenuous and had to be abandoned; the forests seemed interminable; and, to make matters worse, as they drew farther away from Mucozo's tribe, Juan Ortiz had to work through a long chain of translators, each of whom spoke only one dialect besides his own. By the time information had been passed along the line to Ortiz, the result was scarcely intelligible. De Soto was increasingly forced to rely on guesswork to determine his route.

Near the Suwannee River in northern Florida, de Soto finally got the stand-up fight he had been hoping for. A band of some four hundred Indian warriors tried to rescue their chief, who was a hostage in the Spanish camp. After asking for a parley on open ground, they planted an ambush, concealing their weapons in the long swamp grass. De Soto was too experienced a campaigner to be taken in by their offer and decided to spring the trap. Stationing his cavalry in the cover of the surrounding woods, he and several attendants walked out toward the waiting Indians. It was a characteristically brave maneuver, and it paid off. One of de Soto's chief lieutenants, Luis de Moscoso, waited until he saw the savages closing in, then ordered the attack, and the Spanish lancers poured out of the wood, screaming their battle cry. The Indians were caught in their own ambush and could not withstand the horsemen. De Soto swung into the saddle of a spare charger and led the slaughter. Most of the half-naked savages escaped, but some were cut down and a few took refuge by throwing themselves into two small lakes nearby. There they swam out of crossbow range and hurled insults at the white men. De Soto saw his opportunity to teach the enemy a lesson and stationed pickets around the shores. All night long the sentries picked off the Indians as they tried to swim to the bank, using lily pads for camouflage. Next morning

CONTINUED ON PAGE 91

31

Goggles & Side Curtains

By GERALD CARSON

**The roads were terrible, and posted badly or not
at all; you had to equip yourself against a hundred mishaps,
ninety-three of which actually happened—
but you were often up to your hubcaps in pleasure**

In 1900 there were some twenty-one million horses in the United States and fewer than four thousand automobiles. It seemed improbable at the time that the generation then living would witness a reversal of roles. Yet within a quarter of a century Americans would see the end of their long dependence upon animal power as a means of movement.

A Sunday-school teacher in 1920 wound up her account of the Creation by asking the class whether there was any animal that man could have done without. "The horse," said one boy; and the group agreed. Horse history was finished, and Nahum's prophecy in the Old Testament was fulfilled: "The chariots shall rage in the streets," the prophet predicted, "they shall justle [yes, *justle*] one against another in the broad ways: they shall seem like torches, they shall run like the lightnings."

There is no way of saying precisely when the Horse Age ended and the Motor Age arrived. But one can approximate the date. The new era arrived about the turn of the century, when the gasoline vehicle ceased to be experimental and began to *look* like an automobile rather than a buggy directed by a driver sitting on an explosion. The genuine automobile displayed such characteristics of design as a hood, tonneau, and side door; it steered with a wheel instead of a tiller, and was capable of travelling up to forty miles in an hour. If the motor car fell short of Ransom E. Olds's triumphant claim for his Reo, "Nothing to watch but the road," it had at least attained the degree of dependability which made it possible for a young man to do his courting over a radius of fifty miles instead of five, while a proper Bostonian could plan to spend Sunday in the Milton hills with a reasonable expectation of seeing the Common again on the same day.

Lost in the new mobility was the emotional relationship between a man and his horse. But there was a compensating transfer of affection to the sturdy, black, brass-fronted Model T Ford (the "motor car of the

people"), to the popular Overland, or to the stylish Packard ("It gets you there and gets you back"). Men of mature years boasted of the mechanical perfection of their cars, while the young, blithe, and unattached expressed their loyalties in nicknames lettered on the body shell, as in "Galloping Gertrude." Or they decorated the rear with the slogans of the flapper age— "Chicken, Here's Your Roost."

By the second decade of the century the gas auto had won out over the ladylike electric coupé and the slow-starting steamer. The internal combustion engine had been tamed sufficiently to become a practical power plant for a wheeled vehicle steered by a non-professional chauffeur. The family chariot was generally and significantly described in the phrase "pleasure car," and the pleasure it gave was called by the young in heart a "joy ride."

In 1906 Woodrow Wilson, then president of Princeton University, termed the motorcar "a picture of the arrogance of wealth," and declared that "nothing has spread socialistic feeling more than the use of the automobile. . . ." Yet by 1910 it cost less to drive a Maxwell automobile than a horse and buggy—1.8 cents per passenger mile as against 2.5 cents—and by 1924 a new Ford cost no more than a good buggy horse. Instead of resenting the sponsorship of the new machine by the American elite, ordinary citizens learned with satisfaction that "Automobile Red" was very chic, and that Mrs. O. H. P. Belmont considered the "sport" of automobiling "good form." Happily, the rising middle class vowed to emulate such celebrities and social figures as John Jacob Astor, Mark Twain, Chauncey M. Depew, the Vanderbilts, Maude Adams (in her curved-dash Oldsmobile), or Theodore Roosevelt, the first President of the United States to take the wheel of his own car.

Reigning actresses who saw a chance to steal a scene by driving their own roadsters included Lillian Russell, Mrs. Leslie Carter, and Maxine Elliott. Anna

"THE AUTO'S THE PLEASURE FOR ME," 1907

You may sing of life's ma-ny pleas-ures,
Of what-ev-er they may be,
Of boat-ing and bath-ing and base-ball,
But the Au-to's the one for me.
For as it runs a-long smooth-ly,
With-out a jolt or jar,
One might think that they were rid-ing
In a Pull-man Pal-ace car.

Oh some day when life's look-ing drea-ry,
And you're feel-ing migh-ty blue,
Just take a ride out in an Au-to,
And see how it will bright-en you.
It proves to you a re-new-er,
You'll be a boy once more,
And you'll won-der how it hap-pened
How you were so blue be-fore.

Held, fascinatingly French, who helped popularize gum-chewing, challenged any American woman to race her from New York to Philadelphia. There is no evidence that anyone ever accepted the challenge.

The view was widely held, however, during the years when the automobile was being democratized, that women would be passengers but not drivers. They were inclined to hysteria, the argument ran, were not trained to react quickly in the emergencies that would arise in travelling at twenty miles per hour, and in any event would never acquire the knack or the bull strength required to push out the clutch and move the shift stick from low to "intermediate." (What actually happened after skirts were shortened and the electric starter was introduced scarcely requires documentation.)

The theory that women generally would never drive was shattered at an early date in motoring history by the way Miss Alice Roosevelt of the White House went streaking around Washington streets despite the speed limit (twelve miles an hour where there were no trolley tracks, six where there were). Wide attention was focused upon the achievement of Alice Huyler (Mrs. John R.) Ramsey, who in 1909 drove across the continent without a male companion in her thirty-horsepower green Maxwell. And when "two noted suffragists" travelled ten thousand miles in 1914 in their Saxon roadster for the cause of woman's rights, they were, the Saxon people pointed out, "never late once."

One can sense the atmosphere surrounding the automobile, in those yeasty days when touring was first becoming a national pastime, by turning the pages of the popular magazines. They were filled with personal-experience narratives recommending the pleasures of vacationing by automobile: sniff the salt air along the rock-bound coast of Maine; see Mount Rainier's glaciers by moonlight; explore historic Virginia; follow Frémont's route in California for only $1.60 a day.

But first one came up against the problem of a navigable highway. Long-distance travel had been possible only by railway train. Wagon roads were local, used chiefly to move agricultural products from farm to market; they were kept up, if that is the expression, largely by farmers working out their road taxes in lieu of paying cash. Unsurfaced, often unbridged, dusty when dry, filled with bottomless chuckholes in wet weather—holes sometimes maintained by farmers, according to popular rumor, as a source of revenue—the road was often for car and driver the equivalent of

CHORUS:

The au-to's the pleas-ure for me,
The au-to's the pleas-ure for me,
No hill too steep,
No sand too deep,
The au-to's the pleas-ure for me.

35

a gruelling test track. But the resourceful motorist learned the trick of fording an unbridged stream by following a gravel bed leading to the opposite bank. A man of such versatility could also improvise. He knew that when axle-deep in Carolina red clay or the viscous gumbo of the Middle West, the widely available fence rail made an excellent pry for freeing his rear wheels.

Roads were not only next to impassable, they were without signposts; or, at occasional important junctions, there would be a multitude of counsellors, a confusing array of unco-ordinated, pointing wooden fingers. Edmund G. Love, writing of his boyhood in Michigan in his recent book, *The Situation in Flushing,* recalls that his father got stuck in mud holes eight times in one ten-mile stretch between Lapeer and Imlay City, and that he also became hopelessly lost on a detour to Owosso, only twenty miles from home. Towns were seldom identified, since the local citizens knew where they lived. Strangers complained that even the words "U. S. Post Office," where they were displayed at all, were not accompanied by the place name. The embattled farmers—politically strong in state legislatures—contemplating the idea of frightened horses, rising taxes, dead chickens, and stolen fruit, fought a stubborn rear-guard action against better roads or any facilities that would make life more agreeable for automobilists.

By contrast, cyclists were most helpful. The wheeling clubs, which earlier had sprung up everywhere, nourished a new appreciation of mobility. The wheelmen's first tour book, *The American Bicycler* (1880), anticipated the point-to-point automobile manuals, popularized the courtesies of the road, and furnished a pattern for the organization of effective automobile clubs. The cyclists, moreover, established legal precedents regarding the right of a vehicle to use a public highway without the assistance of a horse, as determined by the courts in various decisions in Massachusetts, New Hampshire, and Maine.

In the teens of this century, public pressure for highway improvement became irresistible. "Good Roads" became a slogan—more than that, a "reform," a "movement," even a "gospel." The concept of a continuous, all-weather road across the continent was vigorously promoted by Carl G. Fisher, an Indianapolis manufacturer of carbide-gas lighting equipment for automobiles. The project, known first by the lackluster name of Coast-to-Coast Rock Highway but rechristened in 1913 the Lincoln Memorial Highway,

was dramatized by one of the most massive campaigns of publicity the United States had ever seen. For several years the road remained chiefly an abstraction, a line traced on a map, except for an occasional "seedling mile." In 1916, when there were 3,367,889 automobiles rolling, the Federal Road Aid Act was passed to assist all states that desired to build rural post roads.

The amount of equipment which early motor nomads needed for a journey was astonishing. A partial list, cross-checked against various recommendations, included a rubber lap robe, goggles, tow rope, pump and tire-patching outfit, extra rim lugs, choice of either block and tackle or a winch, reserve cans of gasoline and oil, spotlight, compass, two sets of tire chains, a small length of two-inch plank (to support the jack), and a canvas bucket to fetch emergency water for man and car. Hammacher Schlemmer & Company, the hardware merchants in New York, sold an eighteen-pound Tourist Auto Kit, and the C. A. C. Axle Company in Boston advertised their Damascus Hatchet for special circumstances: "When the wheel drops out of sight in the mud, get out the Damascus, cut a pole for a lever, right things up, and then on your way again." (The uses of a piece of string, a can of ether, and a wad of chewing gum are detailed further on.) Pessimists out for a short spin might also take along tent, sleeping bag, and survival kit.

Father, the family chauffeur, wore a linen duster and, perhaps, Saks & Company's "dignified tourist cap which has attached in the back fold a pair of wide vision goggles cleverly concealed." Feminine passengers in open-car days met the exposure to wind, rain, heat, cold, dust, and mud in charming fashions—ground-sweeping skirts, sleeves shirred at the wrist with elastic bands, cravenette or pongee motor coats, natty turbans, or wide picture hats tied under the chin with demure crepe de Chine bows. "Motor chapeaux," said *Outing,* the outdoor magazine for gentlemen, "frame a pretty face enchantingly."

If the motor girl boggled at the goggles she simply shut her eyes when dust and winged insects swirled around her, and breathed daintily through her handkerchief. Or perhaps her protector was the personal wind shield made by the Auto-Lorgnette Company of Grand Rapids, Michigan, a sort of fan with two panels of transparent celluloid, one clear, the other smoked to shield the eyes from glare. The closed car of the mid-twenties put an end, of course, to these adversities and elegancies.

A need for identifying the car and the owner became

"GIT A HORSE!" 1902

Au-to-mo-bile com-ing down the street,
Git a horse, git a horse;
You will hear this all a-long the beat,
Git a horse, git a horse.
When you're just a-bout to turn a cor-ner,
A rock or something hits you in the ear,
You say your pray'rs and think you are a gon-er,
But soon the say-ing falls up-on your ear:

Git a horse, git a horse,
It's e-nough to make your an-gel broth-er cross.
All the young ones in the land in your path are sure to stand,
Then they dodge away and yell with aw-ful force,
"Git a horse, git a horse."
You're mad e-nough to kill the kids of course.
But a hint to you I'll drop, if you want to make them stop,
Git a horse, git a horse!

apparent as auto thievery replaced horse stealing as a profitable pursuit. During the teens, all states adopted license and registration laws. In New York State in the early days it was up to the operator of the car to provide his own plates, which might be simply a set of old house numbers mounted on a shingle; or he could paint the numbers on the body. Ritzy cars sported white patent-leather tags to which metal numbers were attached, with the pad fixed to the rear axle by straps. Many states found the idea of "foreign" visitors wearing out their roads so distasteful that they erected signs at their boundaries saying "STATE LINE. CHANGE TAGS HERE." Missouri was celebrated for harassment, inhospitality, and red tape. Some counties in the Show-Me state tacked on their own two-dollar fee, while St. Louis charged ten dollars for the use of her streets by Illinoisans. As late as 1914, Maryland still required her neighbors to buy a ticket of admission, and Ohio in 1920 permitted nonresidents to tour the state only if they stayed no longer than a week. Michigan got high marks from the touring public for recognizing out-of-state licenses and allowing speeds of up to twenty-five miles an hour.

Early twentieth-century rural lawmakers tormented the motorist with obscure ordinances. It is reported, but without scholarly confirmation, that one New England town warned drivers: "THE SPEED LIMIT THIS YEAR IS SECRET. VIOLATORS WILL BE FINED $10." Rustic speed cops, certainly, lurked in the bushes; and it is a fact that a Vermont statute once required an automobile to be preceded by a pedestrian carrying a lighted red lantern. Many towns and villages ordered the automobilist to come to a halt when a horse-drawn vehicle approached, or to get out and lead the skittish animal past the offending machine.

Gradually the motor-club movement, brought together in a federalized system of organization under the name of the American Automobile Association, was able to ameliorate the difficulties that harassed the owner of an automobile. The national association was in flourishing condition by the first decade of the century, and projected a vigorous sense of its mission. The A.A.A. concerned itself with such practical matters as better roads, traffic laws, speed traps, reliability runs, and adequate road markers; in addition, it offered its members social activities. Gradually the service concept displaced the socializing. In 1905, to cite a pioneering venture, the Automobile Club of Southern California had a Club Signposting Committee, which was active in marking the roads from Los

Angeles to the beach cities. The next year the club began the posting of El Camino Real ("the king's highway"), the old route of the mission padres between San Diego and San Francisco, with signs depicting large bronze mission bells. Similarly, in 1909, the Chicago Motor Club announced that it had completed installing signs on the roads to Beloit, Lake Geneva, and Milwaukee—except, in the last instance, for fifteen miles that were impassable anyway.

Some manufacturers, too, erected directional signboards at important intersections, each embellished by a discreet advertising notice. Sometimes the advertiser concentrated on his sales message and forgot to supply the information the automobilist needed. A favorite story of the period tells of a motorist lost one rainy night in the wilds of Indiana. Arriving at a fork in the road, he found a sign, but it was placed too high for him to read. He splashed through the sludge, inched up the pole, and tried to light one soggy match after another. The fifth one flared briefly, and by the sputtering light he read, "Chew Red Man Plug."

At about the beginning of World War I, local chambers of commerce and other promotional groups, appraising the growing importance of the travel dollar, joined in the work for better touring conditions. Associations whose total assets often consisted of a map, a letterhead, a few cans of paint, and the spirit of boosterism were formed to direct traffic to one highway rather than another under such catch phrases as "Tightening the Union" or "See America First." Highways were endowed with names that sounded like advertising slogans, which in fact they were, e.g., the Dixie Trail. Many a northern investor hit the Trail to Florida to view the glamorous building lots he had purchased in the land of flowers, oranges, sunshine, and, all too often, swamps. Distinctive bands of paint on telephone poles kept the tourist on his route, pleasantly reminding countless dreamers that they were tooling along in the tradition of the frontiersmen who followed blazed trails through the primeval forest. Main arteries, designated by variegated combinations of stripes and symbols, included the Midland, the Alfalfa, the Cornhusker, the Arrowhead, the Rocky Mountain, the Sunshine, and the Red Ball routes.

"Follow the painted poles," a friendly native would say to a perplexed motorist. "They'll take you right into Chicago!"

"Follow the painted poles?"

"Yes—a white band, with a red streak around the middle. 'R' stands for right turn, 'L' stands for left

CONTINUED ON PAGE 108

"HE'D HAVE TO GET UNDER, GET OUT AND GET UNDER," 1913

He'd have to get un-der, get out and get un-der
To fix his lit-tle ma-chine.
He was just dy-ing to cud-dle his queen,
But ev'-ry min-ute when he'd be-gin it,
He'd have to get un-der, get out and get un-der,
Then he'd get back at the wheel.
A dozen times they'd start to hug and kiss,
And then the darned old en-gine it would miss,
And then he'd have to get un-der, get out and get un-der,
And fix up his au-to-mo-bile.

Rehearsal for

In the fall of 1937, at the entrance of almost any first- or second-class post office in the United States, one was apt to see a Navy poster that showed a fresh-faced young sailor striding up the gangplank of a battleship. Over his shoulder were slung hammock and seabag. On his face was the bright expectation of travel and adventure. And in his pocket, presumably, was the fifty-four dollars a month that a first-class seaman could make in those days.

The picture was an appealing one—but the artist could have made it even more so if he had been depicting a sailor of the United States Navy Yangtze River Patrol. Such a sailor might have been tricked out in natty English walking shorts, a pith helmet, and a full beard. The artist could have shifted the staggering load of canvas on the young man's shoulder to the back of a Chinese coolie following a respectful distance behind. And instead of a battleship, the sailor would have been climbing aboard a gleaming white and mahogany craft nobby enough to run with the brokers' yachts at a Harvard-Yale boat race.

In 1937, except for the dwindling White House flotilla, the Yangtze Patrol was the most comfortable assignment in the Navy. The treaty right to patrol Chinese rivers and territorial waters had been won by the United States, France, Britain, and Russia after they had jointly subdued the terrorist mandarin Yeh in 1858. The duties of the Yangtze Patrol were simple: to watch over the safety and protect the rights and property of American businessmen and missionaries in China. The Patrol had done the job with diligence—and, at times, with cost. It was, however, a job that had its rewards. The quarters, with few exceptions, were light, airy, and unusually comfortable—with bunks for all hands instead of hammocks. Beards were allowed (no other U.S. Navy ships or stations tolerated anything bushier than a pencil-line mustache). Gunboat cooks took great pride in the tables they set: the menus were varied and even exotic, for food prices ashore—graft included—were so universally low that even the most zealous supply officer finally had to wink at the padded cost figures; there was hardly any point in trying to shake up the whole Oriental system for the sake of the Navy's Bureau of Supplies and Accounts.

U.S.S. *Panay,* named after one of the Philippine Islands, had been built in 1927 at Shanghai, along with her sister ship, the *Oahu*. They were two of six gunboats that replaced an ancient fleet of converted yachts and refurbished Spanish-American War prizes. Both ships were specially designed for the Yangtze; they sat low in the water and their drafts were shallow—about five and a half feet. Their bottoms were completely flat, without a trace of a keel. They were likely to roll helplessly in a seaway, but they could ground on a Yangtze sandbar as harmlessly as a soapdish, and could be dragged or floated off equally easily. Seen at a distance running at flank speed in the river, one of the gunboats might appear to be a sinking ship, with decks awash and a captain intent on driving her under in one last, grand gesture. The *Panay* was lightly armed for a ship of war, but gunboats as a class were spawned by a certain damned-if-we-care-if-the-natives-are-restless approach to imperialism; they were intended to fight against an enemy seriously outgunned from the start. On a platform forward and slightly below the bridge, and also on the open upper deck above the stern, the *Panay* carried 3-inch guns mounted behind steel splinter shields thick enough to deflect rifle fire even at close range; sniping from the shore by bandits was a common danger. Both guns were capable of elevating to a

Life aboard the gunboat Panay *was an idyl, and its crewmen were the envy of the fleet. Then, without warning, Japanese bombs started to fall*

By DARBY PERRY

Left: The Panay's *skipper, Lt. Cmdr. James J. Hughes (with binoculars) and three of his officers on the bridge: Lt. Arthur F. Anders, Lt. (j.g.) Clark Grazier, and Ens. Denis H. Biwerse. Right: When the first bombs fell, Hughes was disabled and Anders, his executive officer, took over. After a throat wound left him unable to speak, Anders scribbled orders on the back of this chart, which was soon splattered with his blood. Anders wrote: "Get all small boats alongside. Can we run ship aground if not Abandon Ship." Following pages: These photos of the Japanese attack and the aftermath are stills from movie film shot by Norman Alley of Universal Pictures, who was aboard the* Panay. *They were brought to the U.S. under armed guard and proved that, contrary to Japanese claims, visibility on that day was good.*

On Saturday, December 11, 1937, the Panay lies at anchor above Nanking.

A Panay signalman informs another neutral gunboat that she is about to sail upriver.

At 1:30 P.M. on December 12 the first Japanese plane is spotted overhead.

vertical position for defense against attacking aircraft.

The *Panay*'s upper deck looked like a spacious tropical veranda—except for the presence of light .30 caliber Lewis antiaircraft machine guns. These were also behind heavy, oblong splinter shields that looked a bit like upended water troughs. There were no sights: a good gunner had to have a skeetshooter's instinct for a wing shot.

The *Panay* was built for four officers, forty-nine enlisted men, and a Chinese crew of about a dozen. Behind the bridge the commanding officer, Lieutenant Commander James Joseph Hughes, had a well-appointed two-room suite that served as bedroom, sitting room, dining room, and office. Nearby was a single stateroom occupied by the ship's doctor, Lieutenant (j.g.) Clark Grazier, and the radio room, with transmitters for contact with other ships of the Patrol and with the cruiser *Augusta,* flagship of the Asiatic Fleet, at Shanghai.

The chief petty officers lived in comparably pleasant circumstances on the upper deck astern, the rest of the crew in less capacious quarters on the main deck below. The wardroom and all quarters for officers and enlisted men had big, real windows instead of portholes.

Two thirds of the ship was engine room—under the command of Lieutenant (j.g.) John W. Geist. The powerful twin engines could push the *Panay* at fifteen knots through the spring flood currents that ran like millraces through the Yangtze gorges. Their machinery was tended by an engine-room gang of fifteen sailors and by half a dozen Chinese who wore Navy dungarees, worked like the coolies they were, and lived in the "coolie flat" crammed in under the afterdeck of the port side (starboard was reserved for potatoes). Coolie quarters and pay were not much, but compared to the average coolie's life ashore, the *Panay* provided such luxury that no one worried unduly.

A gunboat might employ just about as many Chinese supernumeraries as the crew could arrange to pay off at the end of the month. They were styled as "boat-men," but held no real rank or official status. They washed, dried, ironed, swept out, scrubbed up, waited table, scoured dishes, polished engines, and ran sampans between ship and shore. A new group could be hired whenever the gunboat moved. The commissary officer was granted a per diem allowance to feed each Chinese boatman, comparable to the allowance provided for other crew members. Since the Chinese wanted—or were presumed to want—little more than rice and vegetables, ninety per cent of their commissary money went to fatten the general mess fund. All dined well.

Good as the food was on board ship, for the officers there was even more sumptuous dining at private homes, clubs, and embassies ashore. The invitations were frequent, and there were sports—riding, shooting, and tennis—to sweat it all out the next day. An officer had only to make the casual remark at noon around the wardroom table that the afternoon was good for tennis —and he would return to his cabin to find his tennis whites and his racket laid out by one of the Chinese.

Involvement in a war seemed highly unlikely, but it was sneaking up fast. In the summer of 1937, charmed by the ease with which it had bitten off Manchuria six years before, Japan had sent 500,000 invading troops to southern China. The resistance had been stouter than most outsiders expected, but by late fall the invaders were closing in on Nanking, the *Panay*'s station, some 225 miles upriver from the coast.

As fall progressed, there had been a number of air raids over Nanking, but the *Panay* had had only one casualty: a crewman coming back from liberty in a state of uncertain stability had fallen overboard and drowned. Most days were routine. As treaty powers or as influential visitors out to "show the flag," most of the nations that would participate in the coming World War had armed ships in the river much of the time, and there was a continual exchange of ceremonial visits and salutes.

As bombs fall, sailors man the Lewis guns. One did not stop to don pants.

Ordered to abandon ship, crewmen toss makeshift rafts overboard and dive in.

Down by the bow, decks awash, the Panay *starts her slow slide to the bottom.*

By December, however, the air raids were coming almost daily, and liberty ashore had been curtailed. All precautions were being taken. The *Panay* now carried two large American flags, each about five feet by nine feet, lashed to the awnings that covered the spacious decks fore and aft. Under way or at anchor she flew her "Sunday flag," the largest ensign in her flag locker; it measured about six by eleven feet. At night all these flags were spotlighted so they could be seen from ashore or aloft. The myth of protective neutrality still hung on from courtlier days of warfare. And the *Panay,* well marked and lighted, was considered a safe refuge—so much so that Chinese shipping tended to squeeze menacingly close to the gunboat when raid alarms sounded.

These things were nuisances, but little more. However, American diplomats knew that the last days of Nanking were likely to be chaotic. When the Chinese troops began to surrender or to try to flee, and when the local government broke down, incidents of looting and dangerous disorder were bound to follow. Early in December, therefore, with the Japanese Army surrounding the city and about to pour over the walls, it seemed prudent to bring embassy personnel out to the ship until Nanking was captured and order was restored. In addition, the *Panay* was already providing refuge for nine American and European businessmen and correspondents.

On Saturday, December 11, the *Panay* and a group of assorted Standard Oil river freighters, motor barges, and launches were anchored close together just above Nanking. At about 2 P.M. some artillery shells that had been directed into the city began to splash around the ships. It could have been poor aim, or a case of mistaken identity. Still, the fire continued. The whole American flotilla got under way—but not before about forty or fifty shells had exploded in the area and one small craft had been damaged. Twelve miles above Nanking the little convoy anchored for the night.

On Sunday morning the trouble started again. Shelling began from the south bank. Possibly it was directed at some junks creeping along the north shore, but Commander Hughes decided to move farther upstream to avoid becoming a chance target for either combatant.

Hughes was a seasoned thirty-nine-year-old regular Navy officer who had been in the service since the summer of 1915 and knew his job well. The movement of the gunboat upstream was to be a routine one. Through diplomatic channels, Hughes asked that Japanese Army units and their armed boats in the river be notified where the *Panay* was moving and why. At 8:25 A.M. Sunday the ship raised anchor and headed upriver again against the sluggish current. The Standard Oil craft, manned by Chinese crews but carrying American or European captains, elected to follow. They, too, were showing American flags. The convoy had been under way only about an hour when Hughes was signalled from the north bank of the river by a Japanese Army unit. At 9:45, as the gunboat lay drifting with a Japanese field piece trained on her from shore, a Japanese lieutenant and a party of six soldiers with fixed bayonets came aboard. Hughes and one of the embassy men were called down from the bridge.

Captain Frank Roberts, the embassy's assistant military attaché, said later that in his opinion the Japanese were intentionally rude, insolent, and high-handed. Hughes and his executive officer, Lieutenant Arthur F. Anders, simply put it down to a poor command of English and sat on their anger. "I had special orders," Hughes explained, "from the Commander Yangtze Patrol not to be too sensitive about points of naval etiquette when dealing with the Japanese military—and above all else, to use my judgment in avoiding such complications as might arise." If there was to be an incident, the Americans were not going to start it.

In broken English the Japanese officer demanded to know if the Americans had seen Chinese soldiers at any point on their trip upriver. Hughes, as protocol dictated, declined to give any information, saying that America was a friend of both China and Japan and could take no part in furthering the military operations of either side. The Japanese then tried to get the captain to come ashore with them. When he refused, they left grudgingly—and the *Panay* got under way again. "At no time," Hughes testified later, "did they indicate we were proceeding into a danger zone."

At about 11 A.M., *Panay* dropped anchor roughly twenty-five miles above Nanking at a spot where the river is about a mile wide, with marshes immediately on either side—ground not likely to attract the operations or stray gunfire of either army. The Standard Oil ships anchored nearby.

Soon after lunch—the Navy's traditional "Sunday dinner"—the lookout on the bridge passed down the word for Commander Hughes that planes were in sight high overhead, coming from upriver. By the time the captain reached the pilot house, picked up a pair of binoculars, and stepped outside to look up, he was astonished to discover the aircraft were losing altitude rapidly as they approached his ship. Almost immediately the planes appeared to go into power dives. Chief Quartermaster John H. Lang shouted a warning, "They're letting go bombs! Get under cover!" He and Hughes ducked back into the pilot house just as the first bomb struck. "It seemed to hit directly overhead," Hughes later recalled. The time was 1:38 P.M.

The radio mast sagged forward at the first bomb burst, and the concussion of other bombs falling knocked people off their feet. The aircraft could be seen plainly now. They were Japanese Navy bombers, the sort that had been used over Nanking. The red suns on their wings stood out clearly.

Ensign Denis H. Biwerse, the *Panay*'s communications officer, saw the first bomb hit. He stepped out onto the port deck forward, glimpsed aircraft, and thought he heard a burst of machine-gun fire; the next thing he knew he was sitting dazed on the deck, his uniform completely blown off except for his shirt, which was in rags. In addition to nearly stripping Bi-

werse, the first bomb had knocked out the bow 3-inch gun, wrecked the pilot house, damaged the radio equipment, ruptured the main fuel line, and wounded the captain severely. "Even though we weren't moving," Engineering Officer Geist said years later, "it was a good shot in those days for a bomber."

Geist headed aft for his battle station. Since the ship was at anchor, his duty was to keep men under cover. As he chased half a dozen gawkers into the crew's shower, he could see three heavy bombers going on downriver. The first three or four bombs had done fatal damage, but now dive bombers were following up the attack. In all, there seemed to be from six to nine planes, coming on in waves of three. "They came low enough for us to see the red suns on their wings distinctly," Geist says, "and we could see the pilots of some of the planes. Even in the excitement, they would have had to see our flags."

The *Panay*'s battery of machine guns had gone into action almost immediately, but mounted as they were, four to a side, they could not easily be trained fully ahead; they were in better position for dealing with snipers on the shore than with dive bombers coming in at 200 miles an hour over the bow. Nevertheless, several of the gunners testified later that they believed several hits were made, "even though not on planes' vital points." Ensign Biwerse, recovering from the concussion of the first bomb, was heading topside toward the radio shack when part of the radio room crumpled in on itself from the blast of another bomb. The mast above it went completely over the side with the same explosion; poor Biwerse was knocked back down the ladder to the main deck.

All the enthusiasm on the part of the *Panay*'s gunners wasn't scaring anyone away. (In a letter to the author, one of the Japanese pilots recently recalled that the *Panay*'s return fire was persistent but, in his words, "somewhat inaccuracy.") "You'd just get rid of one plane and you'd get hit with another," Lieutenant Geist recalled recently. "The bombs were probably hundred pounders. When you get hit square with a

Loaded to the gunwales with men and supplies, a Panay *launch makes shore.*

A wounded Italian reporter, Sandro Sandri, writhes in pain. He died the following day.

Chief Quartermaster John H. Lang was hit in chin and arm, but lived.

couple of hookers like that in a ship the size of *Panay* —which was not much bigger than today's large ocean-going tugs—you can't last long." The Japanese later claimed that they had scored only two direct hits on the *Panay* before they shifted their attack to the cargo vessels, which impressed them as much more appealing targets. But all the ships were close enough together that a near miss on one might inflict casualties on several.

The 3-inch guns were never to get into action. Hughes considered them basically ineffective against aircraft, and regarded the watertight integrity of his ship as far more important than whatever fire could come from these guns. So hatches to the 3-inch magazine stayed dogged tight during the whole fight, and all ammunition for these guns stayed below.

Commander Hughes had a badly fractured right leg, and his face was cut; Dr. Grazier propped him up in the galley, a somewhat protected location. The captain was in considerable pain, and his face was so covered with blood and soot that some of the men recognized him only by the stripes on his sleeve. But he was able to talk to Anders, his executive officer. Anders was suffering from wounds in both hands sustained while loading a machine gun in the first few minutes of the attack. During the second or third bombing salvo he had also been hit in the throat, and he could not speak above a whisper. His orders had to be written on the back of a handy chart (see page 41) or on the white paintwork of the bulkhead. Lieutenant Geist, wounded in the leg, stood by to carry them out.

Twenty minutes or so after the first bomb had dropped, water was a foot and a half deep below decks forward. The pumps were unable to keep up with it. The cabins under the forward gun had been pretty well wrecked by the same blast that disabled the gun. Bridge and radio shack were wrecked. The tiny two-bed sick bay, with most of its supplies, had been riddled—the steel walls shot through with fragments that would have killed anyone who had been in the room. Most of the machine guns were still in action,

but ammunition was running short and water had reached the main magazine below.

Several large holes in the hull along the engine-room and fire-room walls were not only admitting water, but also air. In order to steam, the *Panay*'s fire room had to be put under pressure so there would be a forced draft through the boiler fires. But no pressure could be held with the engine-room bulkheads punctured like good Swiss cheese. Even slipping the anchor chain to try to beach the ship seemed useless; the *Panay* was now so close to the center of the river that she probably would have floated aimlessly with the current for miles —a sitting duck. One of the Standard Oil tankers was under way under her own power and started to maneuver alongside the *Panay* to help, but the *Panay*'s people saw her as a potential floating bomb and waved her off.

At about 2 P.M. Anders passed the order to don life jackets and then pencilled his instructions to Lieutenant Geist on the white bulkhead outside the galley: "Take to the boats. Stay as close to shore as possible. Then swim and send boats back."

The *Panay*'s two launches, both damaged by bullets or bomb fragments, were put over the side. The wounded went in first. Hughes wanted to be allowed to remain in his ship till the last, but Dr. Grazier took advantage of his commander's incapacity to have him carried, protesting, to one of the launches on the second run to shore. The *Panay*'s abandon-ship procedure provided for each of the two small boats to make several trips, each man being assigned to a specific boat and trip. Under the best conditions, it would have taken about thirty minutes to get everyone ashore, but because of the wounded the evacuation was even more difficult and lengthy. Inevitably, there was some confusion. Three crewmen who had given up their life jackets to civilians threw mattresses and table tops over the stern as impromptu rafts and jumped in after them. Roberts, the embassy military attaché (now a retired major general), remembers looking at the 600 yards of cold water between ship and shore and thinking, "I'll never make it." Then the word was passed

CONTINUED ON PAGE 76

Cmdr. Hughes had a badly broken leg, but remained calm and cheerful.

Coolies were recruited to carry the wounded to a friendly Chinese village nearby.

The Panay's *dead were placed aboard another ship and taken to Shanghai.*

PAINTING BY SAMUEL WARD STANTON: THE MARINERS MUSEUM

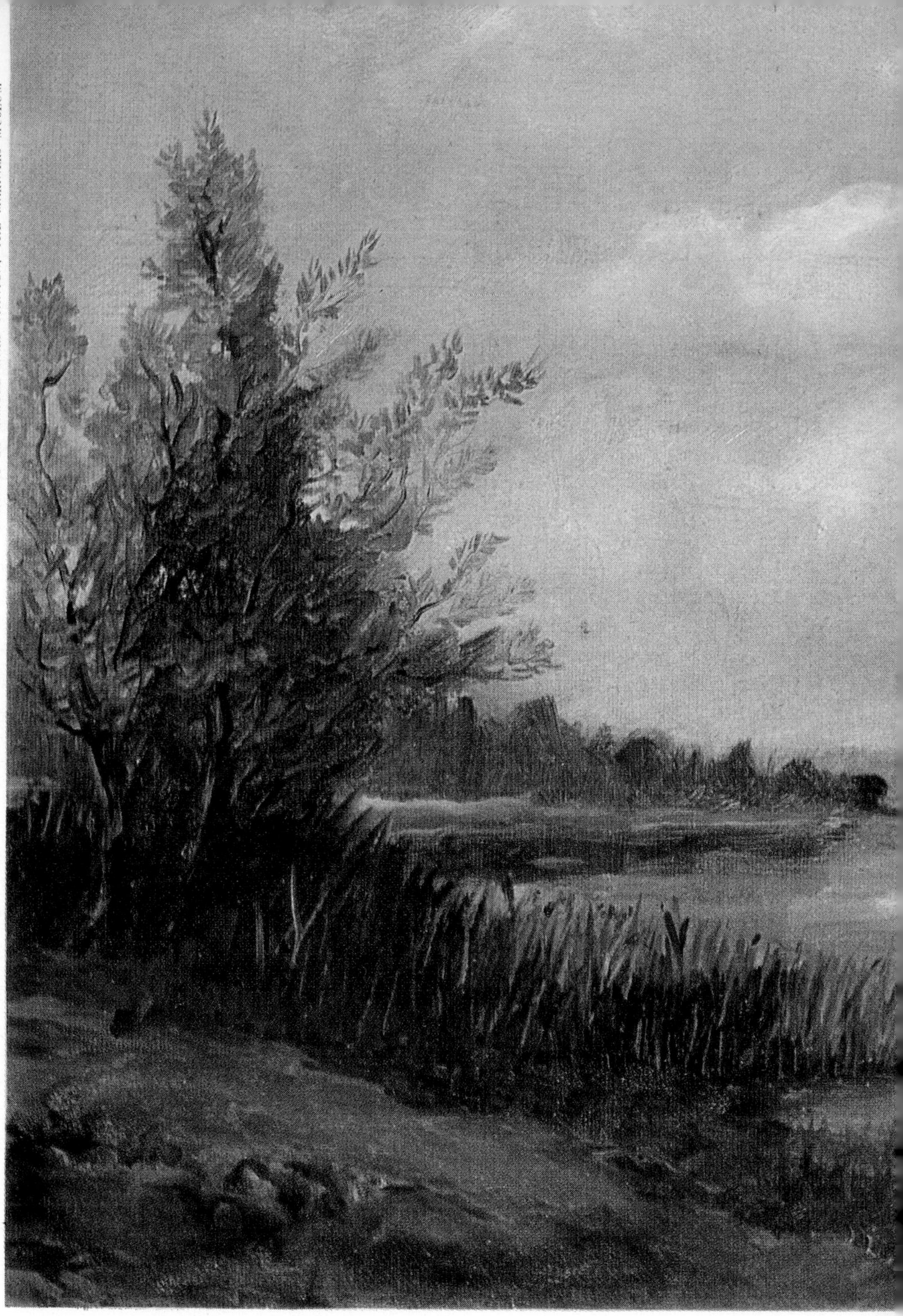

Flowing from the Canadian border to Long Island Sound, nourishing both industry and agriculture, and carrying on its back sailing sloops, steamships, and pleasure craft, the Connecticut River has been for three hundred years

the Main Stream of New England

By ELLSWORTH S. GRANT

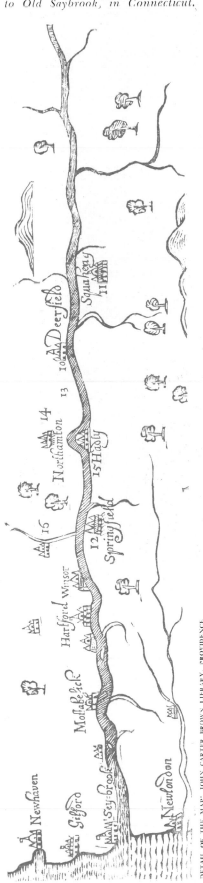

"A river is the most human and companionable of all inanimate things," wrote the famous clergyman-educator Henry van Dyke. "It has a life, a character, a voice of its own." Everyone, therefore, has his favorite stream, from Father Tiber to the mighty Pedernales. Ancient man revered and deified great rivers like the Ganges and the Nile, and along them have grown trade, settlement, and civilization.

The Connecticut River, to be sure, is neither one of the longest nor in any way the most ancient of this great company, but it fits van Dyke's description like a glove. Some artists have thought it compares for beauty, in places, with the Hudson and the Rhine. It is the only body of water

which runs the full length of New England, some four hundred miles from mountain lakes near the Canadian border to Long Island Sound. Once the hunting and fishing grounds of peaceful river Indians—among them the Podunks, Wongunks, and others—then a trading post for the enterprising Dutch, and finally a new territory for land-hungry English settlers, the Connecticut River valley saw many firsts in the history of the new land. Most of these occurred along the seventy miles of riverway within what is now the state of Connecticut. Here were born both the Puritan divine Jonathan Edwards and the inventor of the steamboat, John Fitch; the first cigars, the first canal, the first vessel to engage in the West Indian trade, the first American-built warship (the *Oliver Cromwell,* out of Essex), the first

Left: The idea of self government in Connecticut began with the migration in 1636 of Thomas Hooker and his party from Newtown, near Boston, to what is now Hartford. This Frederick E. Church painting shows Mrs. Hooker on her litter at left, while Hooker himself (at center) encourages one of the women of the group. In the distance, under a bursting sun, is the Connecticut. Above: Trade along the river was begun by William Pynchon, who—also in 1636—brought settlers to the river from Roxbury, Massachusetts. Below: The Charter Oak in Hartford. When in 1687 Sir Edmund Andros, the royal governor, was sent by James II to retrieve the liberal charter granted to Connecticut in 1662, the colonists hid the document in this tree. Had Andros succeeded in seizing it, the seeds of self-government sown by Thomas Hooker might never have borne fruit.

bicycle factory, all these came into being along the Connecticut. The valley is also the home of the oldest continuously published daily newspaper in America, the Hartford *Courant* (originally the *Connecticut Courant*), which dates back to 1764. Perhaps most significant, this is the place where, in drawing up the Fundamental Orders of Connecticut, the founders of the colony brought to birth the world's first written constitution which created a representative government.

The little colony of Connecticut had an impact upon the development of the United States far beyond its size and population. In the nineteenth century, that keen observer of America Alexis de Tocqueville summed up this fact in a speech to Americans celebrating the Fourth of July in Paris in

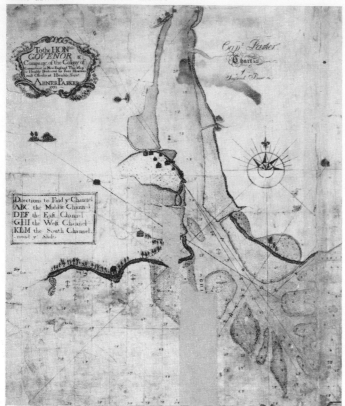

Commerce on the river was held back by tricky sand bars at its mouth, visible in the 1771 map above. In 1773 the merchant Jeremiah Wadsworth (opposite, with his son Daniel) got the Connecticut Assembly to raise money by a lottery—advertised by broadsides (right)—to make navigation both "safe and easy."

1835. Recounting, in his heavily accented English, an illuminating experience he had had in the gallery of the House of Representatives in Washington, he recalled:

...I held one map of the Confederation in my hand. Dere was von leetle yellow spot dey called Connect-de-coot. I found by the Constitution he was entitled to six of his boys to represent him on dat floor. But ven I make de acquaintance person*elle* with de member, I find dat more than tirty of the Representatif on dat floor was born in Connect-de-coot. And then ven I was in the gallery of the House of the Sen*at,* I find de Constitution permits Connect-de-coot to send two of his boys to represent him in dat Legislature. But once more...I find nine of de Senator was born in Connect-de-coot. . . . the leetle yellow spot . . . make de clock-peddler, de school master, and de senator. De first, give you time; the second, tell you what you do with him; and de sird make your law and your civilization.

In his recollection of Tocqueville's remarks, quoted here, the Congregationalist historian William S. Fowler may have made the accent a bit theatrical, but the sentiments are undoubtedly genuine.

But let us return to where the story begins: the river was called the Quinnehtukqut by the Indians, meaning "long estuary" or "long tidal river," because the tide rises and falls as far north as the Enfield rapids, almost at the Massachusetts line, sixty miles from its mouth. The Connecticut twists and eddies through stretches of woods, meadows, and marshes that delight

The Fulton, *whose journey to Hartford made history on the Connecticut River*

the eye of the modern adventurer as much as they must have pleased the Dutch explorer Adriaen Block when he sailed upstream in 1614. Block had been preparing to return to Holland from the island of Manhattan with a cargo of furs when his ship burned. He and his crew then built the *Onrust* (the name means "unrest" or "restless") and continued along the coast to the Connecticut, which he called De Versche, "the Freshwater" river. (The explorer is memorialized by Block Island, just outside the point where Long Island Sound meets the Atlantic.)

In the state to which it gave its name the river varies in width from 600 to 2,100 feet; it is creased with shifting shoals that have always made navigation difficult for all but vessels with the shallowest draft, while the sand bar at its exit into the sound—formed by the conflux of river and tidal currents—prevents any great port from rising at its mouth. The historian Benjamin Trumbull once observed that "as its banks are generally low, it forms and

PAINTING BY P. FUERSTENBERG; WADSWORTH ATHENEUM

After the Fulton *churned up the river in 1815, steam swiftly replaced sail along the Connecticut. Sailing vessels like the* Cleopatra *(below), built on the river in the late 1700's, were clumsy in the confined channels. They gave way to small, shallow-draft stern-wheelers like the* Barnet *and, later, to big boats like the famed* City of Hartford, *seen at left passing Goodspeed's famous hotel in East Haddam about 1850.*

The Barnet, *which in 1826 became the first boat to go 200 miles upriver*

fertilizes a vast tract of the finest meadow," the unique sandy soil of which proved ideal for growing the Indian plant called tobacco, still an important crop in the Connecticut Valley. Especially in the last thirty miles of its course the river is an impressive spectacle: the rugged cliffs of the Middletown Straits, the gentle hills that turn purple in the twilight, the tree-covered islets, and everywhere the quiet villages with their tall white church spires and gracious homes built by river captains and merchants.

Immense schools of fish once populated the river. Salmon were so plentiful in colonial days that it was prohibited to feed them to bond servants more than thrice weekly. During the spawning season, one legend has it, a man with snowshoes could cross the river on their backs. In Old Saybrook's South Cove one Elias Tully caught 3,700 salmon in one haul. Herring, striped bass, and shad also ran in great numbers. The latter sold for as little as a penny apiece, and people who would eat them were consid-

53

Above: The metropolis of the river is Hartford, capital of the Land of Steady Habits and center of the American insurance industry. Like most river towns it has suffered much from the freshets and floods which have occurred with devastating regularity since the first to be recorded, in 1635. This one took place in 1855 and was painted by Joseph Ropes for Hartford arms maker Samuel Colt, who was for years the biggest employer along the river.

WINDSOR

HADDAM

ered of pretty mean estate. Indians fertilized their cornfields with shad, but later the ingenious colonists found a market for them by salting and packing the fish in hogsheads and shipping them as far as Portugal.

What attracted the white man to the Connecticut River valley was, first of all, trade and, soon after, land. Block's voyage upstream as far as the Enfield rapids had resulted in the exchange of goods for beaver pelts which the Indians had brought downriver in their long narrow dugouts. But no sooner had the Dutch erected—in 1633—a little fort and trading post called House of Hope, just below the present site of Hartford, than the English, both by sea and land, descended upon the valley. At the same time that the Pequots, a warlike division of the Mohegan, were making the initial sale of riverfront property to the Dutch (for, it is said, "1 piece of duffel . . . , 6 axes, 6 kettles, 18 knives, one sword blade, 1 pr. of shears, some toys, and a musket"), Podunk sachems were journeying to Boston and Plymouth to solicit English settlers with promises of corn and beaver skins and glowing descriptions of the "exceeding fruitfulness of the country." What the Indians along the river wanted was protection against the hostile neighboring Pequots. The bait was taken when, in the fall of 1633, William Holmes and his followers settled at what became Windsor, Connecticut.

During the next few years groups from Massachusetts led by Thomas Hooker and others made settlements along the river at Hartford and Wethersfield. Thus was established the nucleus of the Connecticut colony. One eminent historian, Charles M. Andrews, maintains, in the face of some skepticism, that "every acre . . . was honestly obtained." In any case, the land was worthless to the unwarlike river tribes without the Englishman's musket. Soon the settlers and their Indian friends had to contend with and later decimate the Pequots. Eventually most of the red men disappeared

Below: Here and on the page opposite are engravings of four famous Connecticut River towns. Enfield, near the Massachusetts line, was the site of the famous rapids. Windsor, just north of Hartford, has long been a tobacco center. Haddam, only thirty miles from the mouth of the river, once thrived on the shad-fishing industry. Old Lyme, near the sound, was a port where "a sea captain once lived in every house."

before the onslaught of the white man's diseases and the conversion of their hunting and fishing paradise into a land of villages and cultivated fields. Now the English had only the Dutch to deal with.

Considering their different objectives, it was inevitable that the English in their new settlements and the Dutch in their little fort would clash. Rarely on the frontier have agricultural and trading societies been able to live peacefully together. Out of this confrontation came the word that is now universally applied to citizens of the United States, "Yankee." It probably derives from the Dutch diminutive of Jan, Janke (Johnny in English), and then, as now, one of the implications of the term was "rascal" or "brigand." It was a common nickname among the Dutch buccaneers along the Spanish Main. Thus, it was natural for the Dutch traders to brand the Englishmen who coveted the rich meadowland around their post *janke* pirates.

With families to feed, the Yankee newcomers soon commenced to encroach on Dutch territory, planting life-giving corn and other crops. The Dutch were too few and the English multiplying too fast for the struggle to be even; unable to resolve their legal claims and unwilling to risk open warfare, the Hollanders finally sailed downriver for good in 1654. A hundred years later the Yankee, by then a trader par excellence, was the butt of jokes everywhere he appeared. But he always bore proudly the nickname which had come to connote, in addition to "rascal," one who was shrewd, inventive, and practical; and some would proclaim, as did the hero of Mark Twain's *A Connecticut Yankee in King Arthur's Court:* "I am an American. I was born and reared in Hartford, in the state of Connecticut. . . . So I am a Yankee of the Yankees. . . ."

One of the warmest debates over American history has been centered around the question of whether or not Thomas Hooker's concept of govern-

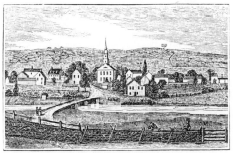

ENFIELD

OLD LYME

PAINTING BY CARLETON WIGGINS; COLLECTION OF RICHARD F. COOPER

Agriculture and industry have a long history in the Connecticut Valley. Tobacco fields like those at Middletown (opposite page, top) have been cultivated since the late 1700's. Farming is still important, though primitive ferries like the one carrying hay in Old Lyme, shown in the nineteenth-century painting above, no longer run. Shipyards were once common; the one at Deep River (lower left) was photographed in 1866. Brownstone for many houses in New York, Boston, and Philadelphia came from quarries at Portland (below).

ment and the Fundamental Orders which he persuaded the Connecticut colonists to adopt in 1639 were really democratic. It is undoubtedly too much to claim that they were democratic in the modern sense of the word. Hooker's departure from Massachusetts was primarily motivated by a desire, not to abolish the Puritan state, but to found a less rigidly theocratic one of his own. Hooker's ideas were much closer to our modern notions than were those prevalent in Massachusetts Bay. "The foundation of authority," Hooker theorized, "is laid, firstly, in the free consent of the people." Even if by "people" Hooker meant the "admitted inhabitants" and freemen who were competent, church-going Congregationalists and land owners, his scheme was much more inclusive than that of the Boston theocrats who limited the control of government to those few church members who were, in their eyes, "spiritually elect."

Affairs in Connecticut towns were initially conducted by committees appointed in a meeting of the whole electorate; later this function was taken over by elected town officers, subsequently called selectmen. In practice, a very few men—ministers, merchants, and lawyers from the leading families,

WETHERSFIELD HISTORICAL SOCIETY

Yesterday... *In the nineteenth century the Connecticut was a corridor of unspoiled beauty. In 1836 Thomas Cole captured the grandeur of its middle reaches in* The Oxbow, *right, a depiction of the river's loop at Northampton, Massachusetts. The painting above shows the sloop* Hornet *passing Saybrook light, at the river's mouth, about 1885.*

the so-called Standing Order—controlled the government well into the nineteenth century. Town meetings were held monthly, called at nine in the morning by the beating of a drum or the blowing of a trumpet from the top of the meeting house. Since the same building was used for both religious and civic functions, practically speaking Church and State were one until the constitution of 1818 disestablished the Congregational Church as the state-supported religion. But the town meeting survives: 118 of Connecticut's 169 towns retain this form of self-rule.

The next settlement after the three original river towns was Saybrook, which played a leading role in the river's history because of its strategic location near the mouth. In 1635 a group of Puritan lords, having obtained a grant from Robert Rich, Earl of Warwick, to the Saybrook territory, sent over a tough but fair-minded soldier and military engineer, Lion Gardiner, at a salary of 100 pounds per annum, to build a fort and take charge of the defenses of the colony. In April, 1636, during an Indian siege, a son was born to Gardiner and his Dutch wife, the first recorded birth of a white child in the colony. William Fiennes, First Viscount Saye and Sele, and Robert Greville, Lord Brooke, and their fellow adventurers hoped to make Saybrook a Puritan refuge from royal persecution. But though a number of prominent Puritans were interested in the scheme, only George Fenwick and his lovely redheaded lady, Alice, ever came to claim their share of the land. The Fenwicks' dream of building a manor house was shattered by the marauding Pequots, while the fickle sandbar at the river's mouth spoiled their plan of making Saybrook Point a port.

Finally, in 1644, Fenwick sold the fort to the General Court at Hart-

CONTINUED ON PAGE 100

...and Today

58

For ten tumultuous years Sam Adams burned with a

single desire: American independence from Great Britain

FIREBRAND *of the* REVOLUTION

By ALEXANDER WINSTON

embers of the British Parliament who voted approval of the Stamp Act late one night in 1765 and went yawning off to bed had never heard, it would seem, of Boston's "Man of the Town Meeting," Samuel Adams. It was a fatal lapse. From that moment until the Declaration of Independence, Sam Adams pounced on Britain every time she moved to impose her will on the colonies. He made politics his only profession and rebellion his only business. He drove two royal governors out of Massachusetts and goaded the British government into open war. New England Tories branded him the "grand Incendiary," the "all-in-all" of colonial turmoil, and neatly capsuled Boston resistance as "Adams' conspiracy." In the opinion of his astute cousin John Adams, Sam was "born and tempered a wedge of steel to split the knot of *lignum vitae* that tied America to England."

"Born and tempered," as Cousin John put it, was more than rhetorical flourish. Sam's father—also named Samuel—made an avocation of politics, and was suspected of republican leanings. The boy got a taste for public affairs almost with his milk; while he was but a toddler his father was deep in the Caucus Club, the same radical brotherhood that Sam was to use with such adroitness. Sam senior clashed with royal governors, and venture—an eff tiable paper Parliament tion that and unj Fro Calvi

with Britain resemble a huge and murky illustration for *Paradise Lost.* The American patriots, Sam was sure, were children of light who fought England's sons of Belial in a struggle decisive for the future of mankind. Everyone knew where God stood on that. Sam saw England through a glass, darkly: her government venal, her manners effeminate and corrupt, her religion popish. In saving the colonies from her tyranny Sam hoped to save their manly virtues as well, and make of Boston a "Christian Sparta"—chaste, austere, godly. By 1765 three dominant strains were firmly fixed in his character: puritanism, political acumen, and hatred of British rule. He laced them together tight as a bull whip and, as Parliament was to discover, twice as deadly.

Any calm appraisal of his life up to that point, however, would surely have rated him among those least likely to succeed. After Harvard (M.A., 1743) he had dabbled at the study of law and later spent a few fruitless months as apprentice in a countinghouse. His father loaned him a thousand pounds to make a try at business—any business. The money ran through his fingers like water. Appointed Boston's tax collector in 1756, he combined softheartedness and negligence so ably that he ended at least four thousand pounds in arrears and faced court action. The prosperous little had left the family fell to ouse for was the Caucus Club, a judicious mixture of shipyard laborers ("mechanics") and uptown intellectuals. They met in a garret to drink punch, turn the air blue with pipe smoke, and plot the next political move. Their decisions were passed quietly along to other radical cells—the Merchants' Club (which met in the more genteel Boston Coffee House), the contentious Monday Night Club, the Masons, the Sons of Liberty. With tactics mapped out and support solidified, the action was rammed—or finessed, if need be—through town meeting. Nothing was left to chance; Sam and his tight coterie of patriots simply outworked, outmaneuvered, and, on occasion, outlasted the opposition.

At first rumor of the Stamp Act, Sam cried that "a deep-laid and desperate plan of imperial despotism has been laid, and partly executed, for the extinction of all civil liberty." But Parliament considered its act perfectly just. England's recent conquest of Canada, which had removed an armed threat to the colonies from the French, had also run up a burdensome debt. Obviously the colonies, who had benefited most from the costly Canadian expedition, should not mind paying part of the bill. Passed in the spring of 1765, the Stamp Act required that after November 1 of that year validating stamps be bought from government offices and affixed to all legal documents, customs papers, newssheets, and pamphlets. To enforce the act Parliament decreed that offenders be tried in admiralty courts, where there were no juries, and pay their fines in silver coin, which was hard to get.

Sam rolled out his artillery months before the act went into effect. The instructions from the Boston town meeting to its representatives in the Massachusetts House constituted one of the first formal protests made in the colonies against the act, and one of the first appeals for united resistance. Sam declared that since the act imposed taxation by a body in which the taxed were not represented it flouted the Massachusetts charter, violated the established rights of British subjects, and was therefore null and void.

On the morning of August 14, 1765, the effigy of old Andrew Oliver, Boston distributor of stam[...] from the Liberty Tree [...] Sam in[...]

day "the People shouted; and their shout was heard to the distant end of this Continent." Two weeks later rioters sacked and gutted the mansion of Lieutenant Governor Thomas Hutchinson, emptying his wine cellar and scattering his papers in the street.

On November 1, 1765, the day the Stamp Act went into effect, church bells tolled as for the dead. Flags hung at half-mast; from the harbor rolled the dull boom of minute guns. For the next six weeks the people of Boston refused to buy stamps. Port business came to a halt, law courts tried no cases. Sam had warned the farmers: "If our Trade may be taxed why not our Lands? Why not the Produce of our Lands and in short everything we possess or make use of?" He doubly damned the stamp revenue by prophesying that it would be used to fasten an episcopacy on puritan New England. In the provincial House, to which he had been elected in September, Sam had a gallery installed to bring waverers under the accusing eye of his patriots. He and his colleague James Otis published a black list of those House members whose antagonism to the act lacked proper vigor. Frightened stamp officials fled for protection to Castle William in the harbor. Enforcement collapsed, and early in the next year Parliament repealed the act. But Sam did not join in Boston's celebration. Why rejoice, he grimly demanded, when Parliament has only granted us our just due?

The defeat of the Stamp Act suggested that no one in the colonies could hatch and execute a scheme with half Sam's cunning. His strategy was to let Britain make all the moves and then give her a bloody nose. "It is a good maxim in Politicks as well as War," he counselled, "to put and keep the enemy in the wrong." Britain soon obliged again. In May, 1767, Parliament launched a series of colonial bills named for their sponsor, Charles Townshend, Chancellor of the Exchequer. The Townshend Acts placed import duties on painters' colors, glass, lead, paper, and tea. At the same time they set up Commissioners of Customs with broad powers, authorized search warrants, and specified that the revenue would be used to pay Crown [...] salaried (and therefore in part con[...] [...]ion as the chief [...] 1769 all the [...] revelled in [...]titutional

[...]ed with
[...] shows
[...]ernor
[...]roops
[...]1768.

power is drawn round this bundle of arrows, the *firmer* it will be."

To enforce the boycott in Boston, gangs ranged outside the homes of Tory merchants by night, and small boys pelted their customers with dirt and dung by day. One shopkeeper, more obstinate than the rest, was ridden out of town to the gallows and loosed only when he swore never to return. Tories slept with loaded pistols by their beds. Governor Francis Bernard pleaded for military protection, and in September of 1768 two regiments of soldiers sailed in from Halifax. They set up guardposts, and levelled a pair of cannon at the town hall.

Overnight Governor Bernard became the most hated man in Massachusetts. The House demanded his removal; at Harvard, students slashed his portrait. Sam denounced him as "a Scourge to this Province, a curse to North America, and a Plague on the whole Empire." Recalled to England, Bernard sailed at the end of July, 1769, leaving Hutchinson to act as governor in his place. Despite Sam's outraged cry that Boston was now an occupied town, the troops remained, and he began sending a periodic *Journal of Events* to other colonies, accusing the redcoats of beating defenseless boys and raping women.

Early in March, 1770, a soldier was injured in a scuffle with dockmen. One morning soon after, the town was plastered with forged notices, allegedly signed by redcoats, promising a broad-scale attack on the townspeople. That night, March 5, as a bright moon shone on the late snow, a crowd gathered in front of the Custom House. It began to taunt the nine-man guard; snowballs and brickbats flew, the guard fired, and five citizens were left dead or dying.

The town was in a frenzy of anger. On the following afternoon an immense rally of excited citizens massed in and around Old South Church. Hutchinson told a committee of protest that he was willing to send the one offending regiment to the fort at Castle William but that he had no military authority to send the other as well. At dusk Sam came to the State House to deliver his ultimatum: "If you ... have the power to remove *one* regiment you have the power to remove *both*. It is at your peril if you refuse. The meeting is composed of three thousand people. They are become impatient. A thousand men are already arrived from the neighborhood, and the whole country is in motion. Night is approaching. An immediate answer is expected. Both regiments or none!" Hutchinson caved in and ordered the two regiments out of town.

Sam relished his moment of triumph. "If Fancy deceive me not," he reported, "I observ'd his Knees to tremble. I thought I saw his face grow pale (and I

enjoy'd the Sight)." Copley's fine portrait (see page 63) catches Sam at the moment of confrontation: broad forehead, heavy eyebrows, steady blue-gray eyes, nose like the prow of a ship, stubborn mouth, a chin you could plow with.

Sam wanted the soldiers who had fired the fatal shots to be tried immediately, while indignation still flamed white-hot, but the judges put it off for six months. He acquiesced when two patriots, his cousin John and Josiah Quincy, volunteered to be defense attorneys, sure that they would not press too hard on prosecution witnesses. The two proved more honorable than he had counted on; they argued their case ably and the sentence was light—a pair of soldiers were branded on the thumb. Sam was disgusted. He retried the case in the Boston *Gazette,* over the signature "Vindex," the avenger. (For a full account of the Boston Massacre trial, see AMERICAN HERITAGE, December, 1966.)

After that, to Sam's chagrin, things quieted down. The blood of the "massacre" had washed away with the melting snow. In England a liberal government had assumed power and in April it repealed the Townshend Acts, except for the duty on tea. A majority of the colonists were tired of agitation, and the radical patriots temporarily lost control of the Massachusetts House. John Hancock courted the royalists; John Adams shook the dust of politics from his shoes and went back to pastoral Braintree. James Otis, who had been bludgeoned in a brawl, sank into recurrent fits of dementia.

Only Sam never let up. "Where there is a Spark of patriotick fire," he vowed, "we will enkindle it." Between August, 1770, and December, 1772, he wrote more than forty articles for the *Gazette*. Night after night, a lamp burned late in the study off his bedroom. Friends, passing in the small hours, could look up at the yellow square of window light and comfort themselves that Sam Adams was busily at work against the Tories. Sam alternately stated the fundamentals of colonial liberty (based on the charter, British law, and, finally, natural right) and whiplashed the British for transgressing it. His style in this period was at times severely reasoned, more often impassioned; the content was unfailingly polemical, partisan, and, on occasion, willfully inaccurate. As the conflict with Britain deepened, his accusations became more violent. "Every dip of his pen," Governor Bernard had once said, "stung like a horned snake." As clerk of the House (to which office he had been elected in 1765) Sam poured out a stream of remonstrances, resolves, and letters to the colony's London agent; but beyond their effect as propaganda he expected them to do little good. When his daughter expressed awe that a petition

CONTINUED ON PAGE 105

64

gressman "a person of notorious profligacy of life ... a certain disgrace has for years past attended the reputation of being one of his companions ... the man who in his own practice regards adultery as a joke and the matrimonial bond as no barrier against the utmost caprice of licentiousness—has little right to complain when the mischief which he carries without scruple into other families enters his own."

Also in New York, George Templeton Strong confided to his not-yet-famous diary, "Were he [Sickles] not an unmitigated blackguard and profligate, one could pardon any act of violence committed on such provocation. But Sickles is not the man to take the law into his own hands and constitute himself the avenger of sin."

Others recalled how Sickles in his bachelor days had squired a luscious courtesan named Fanny White around town; she even accompanied him to Albany when he was elected to the state assembly. Less certain was the rumor that after his marriage, when he left his pregnant wife in New York to go to London with Buchanan, Sickles took Fanny White along and insolently introduced her to Queen Victoria. From his earliest days in Tammany, Sickles had had

While his friend Butterworth watches appreciatively, Sickles gives the protesting Philip Barton Key the coup de grâce.

67

*Most love triangles prob-
ably ought to be represented
with two acute angles and one
obtuse. In this case it would not be
easy to say whether the obtuse corner
was occupied by the handsome Philip Barton Key (left), who almost publicly flaunted
his affair with Teresa Bagioli Sickles, or by the
fiery Dan Sickles (right), who despite his tremendous
savoir faire* seemed to be the last person in Washington
to learn what was going on. But there is no doubt who was
at the apex of the triangle: the sultry Teresa, whom both gentlemen passionately loved and who, it seems, amply responded.

a reputation as a brawler, ready to attack or defend with fists, pistols, or bowie knife. This, and a consistent disdain for paying his debts, had him frequently in court. The more people remembered, the more unlikely became Dan Sickles' posture as a defender of marital fidelity.

The first and most crucial move was in the hands of the prosecution. Would solemn District Attorney Ould attack in his opening statement only Sickles' crime—the fact of homicide which the defense could hardly deny—or would he include the character of the defendant? Undoubtedly Messrs. Brady, Graham, and Stanton breathed a subtle sigh of collective relief when Ould proceeded to concentrate his fire on the deed. In vivid terms Ould underscored the armed power of the assailant and the helplessness of the unarmed victim, also noting that Sickles chose Sunday to accomplish his "deed of blood." The prosecuting attorney called the Congressman "a walking magazine, a temporary armory, a moving battery . . . like a piece of flying artillery on a field of battle." He pictured Key as in poor health, and armed with nothing but an opera glass which he vainly flung at Sickles when the assault began. This, Ould solemnly declared, was "murder, no matter what may be the antecedent provocation in the case." The prosecution now proceeded to summon a parade of witnesses who titil- lated the courtroom with hair-raising recollections of the murder scene. James H. Reed, a wood and coal dealer, told how Key took cover behind a tree after the first shot (which apparently missed), then crumpled to the ground after the next shot and was hit a second time while lying

on the pavement begging, "Don't shoot." Except for the flung opera glass, there was no evidence of any resistance by the terrified victim.

But Washington and the press were more astonished by the District Attorney's failure to call another witness— Samuel F. Butterworth. A Tammany sachem, Butterworth had happened to be in Washington on political business when Sickles discovered the truth about his wife and Key. Butterworth had called on Sickles in response to a note asking his advice on what course the injured husband should take. As they talked, Key appeared in Lafayette Square and began making signals toward the Sickles house with his handkerchief. It was Butterworth who rushed out of the house alone and detained Key long enough for Sickles to go upstairs, find and load both his derringer and a revolver, and rush out to kill him. Butterworth would have been a hostile witness, and Ould knew that if he called him to the stand he would be legally barred from cross-examining him; but a first-class attorney would have taken the risk because the mere fact of Butterworth's actions cast an aura of calculation over the crime—the very point for which Ould was contending. Instead, Ould let the defense seize the initiative and ask the court to *re- quire* the prosecution to put Butterworth on the stand, as well as an even closer friend of Sickles', George Wool- dridge, who was in the Congressman's house when the murder was committed.

A lively argument ensued. Carlisle, Ould's associate, maintained that the defense was making this demand to win "the pleasant cross-examination of the counsel for the prisoner, and protect [Butterworth and Wooldridge] from what might be the unpleasant cross-examination of the counsel for the prosecution." Seventy-three-year-old Judge Thomas H. Crawford, described by one lawyer as "a sharp-featured old gentleman with a bald head somewhat shaped like that of a chicken," ruled it was not necessary for "the United States" to bring Butterworth and Wooldridge to the stand, since more than enough witnesses had already been produced to describe the bloody deed. But Sickles' lawyers had made their point. By getting the prosecution to back away from Butterworth they had in effect cancelled him out as a threat to their client. They then comfortably ignored him for the rest of the trial, and only later did the prosecutors and the public learn that Mr. Butterworth had left town before the proceedings began.

The defense also showed their coolness under fire when the prosecution placed in evidence the derringer pistol and ball that had killed Key. James T. Brady blithely noted that while the bullet had been positively identified as the one that killed Key, no one on the prosecution side had identified the gun. In a burst of verbal gymnastics Brady implied that the murder weapon might belong to Key, an assertion that brought outraged gasps from the prosecution.

Ould's performance had been feeble, but he nevertheless rested his case, and the defense opened with a thunderous oration by John Graham. In rolling, ponderous periods, Graham seized on Ould's sarcasm about Sickles' profanation of the Sabbath and converted it into a bludgeon of defense. Who had profaned the Sabbath, the injured husband or "a confirmed, habitual adulterer . . . besieging with most evil intentions that castle where for their security and repose the law had placed the wife and child of his neighbor"? Sickles, Graham contended, was acting in self-defense when he killed Key. No matter that under the law of the District of Columbia a wronged husband could sue an adulterer for damages. The law, he said, was almost ludicrously inconsistent on this point. "If an individual comes into your house and lies upon your bed against your will, he commits a trespass and you can repel him by force. If an individual comes into your house and lies with your wife and robs her and you of that which cannot be restored and for which no recompense can be made, can you not repel this invasion by force? Can your wives be used with impunity when your furniture cannot?" There was only one possible answer to this contradiction, thundered Graham. "If society has not protected you in the possession of your wives, it is proof conclusive that society meant that your right to their possession should remain as at nature and that the right to protect the purity of your wives is a natural right which you can assert, even to the extent of killing whoever seeks to deprive you of it, as much as you can kill for the purpose of protecting your own lives." It is, he declared, a right "given by the law of God."

Quoting Shakespeare, the Bible, and judicial examples ranging all the way back to the Roman Empire, Graham elaborated this defense of the "higher," or "unwritten," law. He combined a shrewd use of the Bible and his own wits to plug up the most obvious hole in Sickles' case—his failure to kill Key for two full days after an anonymous letter had informed him that the District Attorney had made him a cuckold. Pointing out that Absalom waited two full years to kill the violator of his sister, Graham proceeded to argue that if the law permits a husband to kill an adulterer caught in the act, it is equally permissive if the seducer is caught "so near the act as to leave no doubt as to his guilt." Was this not precisely what had happened between Sickles and Key? The Congressman did not invite the debonair district attorney to stroll past his house on that fatal Sunday afternoon and wave his adulterous handkerchief at Mrs. Sickles' window. "Is it possible that under these circumstances," Graham asked the jury, "Mr. Sickles could have acted in cold blood?" Indeed, he went on, Sickles' provocation was so enormous that he was, from a legal point of view, insane. Graham proceeded to dwell on Key's professed or avowed friendship with Sickles; he pointed out that Key had retained his job as district attorney largely because Sickles had interceded with President Buchanan for him. With heavy sarcasm he emphasized the hypocrisy of Key's private conduct when contrasted to his public station. Finally, Graham stressed two cases: in 1843 a New Jersey jury acquitted one Singleton Mercer, charged with killing the man who had raped his sister; more recently in a Washington criminal court trial presided over by the same Judge Crawford and prosecuted, ironically, by the late Philip Barton Key, the jury had acquitted one Jarboe for exacting the same revenge for a similar reason.

Graham talked for almost two full days, a feat even in an era of massive eloquence. His performance drastically altered the trial's center of gravity. Thereafter the defense was in possession of the initiative, while Ould and Carlisle found themselves playing the unpleasant role of obstructionists.

This became sensationally apparent when Brady attempted to place in evidence the trial's *pièce de résistance* —the confession that Congressman Sickles had extracted from his tearful, hysterical wife the night before he killed Key, after detective work by his friend George Wooldridge had convinced him that she was guilty. Bridget Duffy, Mrs. Sickles' maid, identified the paper, written in her mistress' hand, and told how the confession was produced after an angry scene punctuated by shouts and cries in Mrs. Sickles' bedroom. At the Congressman's request, Bridget had signed it as a witness, and a young woman friend of Mrs. Sickles', Octavia Ridgeley, had done likewise.

"This paper," Brady declared, "we propose to read in evidence. It is Mrs. Sickles' statement to her husband:

" 'I have been in a house in 15th Street with Mr. Key. How many times I don't know. I believe the house belongs to a colored man. The house is unoccupied. Commenced going there the latter part of January. Have been in alone with Mr. Key. Usually stayed an hour or more. There was a bed in the second story. I did what is usual for a wicked woman to do. The intimacy commenced this winter when I came from New York, in that house—an intimacy of an improper kind. Have met half a dozen times or more at different hours of the day. On Monday of this week. And Wednesday also. Would arrange meetings when we met in the street and at parties. Never would speak to him when Mr. Sickles was at home, because I knew he did not like me to speak to him; did not see Mr. Key for some days after I got here. He then told me he had hired the house as a place where he and I could meet. I agreed to it. Had nothing to eat or drink there. The room is warmed by a wood fire. Mr. Key generally goes first. Have walked there together say four times—I do not think more; was there on Wednesday last, between two and three. I went there alone. Laura was at Mrs. Hoover's. Mr. Key took and left her there at my request. From there I went to 15th Street to meet Mr. Key; from there to the milk woman's. Immediately after Mr. Key left Laura at Mrs. Hoover's I met him in 15th Street. Went in by the back gate. Went in the same bedroom, and there an improper interview was had. I undressed myself. Mr. Key undressed also. This occurred on Wednesday, 23rd of February, 1859.

" 'Mr. Key has kissed me in this house [*i.e.*, the Sickles house on Lafayette Square] a number of times. I do not deny that we have had a connection in this house last spring, a year ago, in the parlor on the sofa. Mr. Sickles was sometimes out of town and sometimes in the Capitol. I think the intimacy commenced in April or May, 1858. I did not think it safe to meet him in this house, because there are servants who might suspect something. As a general thing, have worn a black and white woollen plaid dress and beaver hat trimmed with black velvet. Have worn a black silk dress there also, also a plaid silk dress, black velvet cloak trimmed with lace, and black velvet shawl trimmed with fringe. On Wednesday I either had on my brown dress or black and white woollen dress, beaver hat and velvet shawl. I arranged with Mr. Key to go in the back way after leaving Laura at Mrs. Hoover's. He met me at Mr. Douglas's. The arrangement to go in the back way was either made in the street or at Mr. Douglas's as we would be less likely to be seen. The house is in 15th Street between K and L Streets on the left-hand side of the way; arranged the interview for Wednesday in the street, I think, on Monday. I went in the front door, it was open, occupied the same room, undressed myself and he also;

went to bed together. Mr. Key has ridden in Mr. Sickles' carriage and has called at his house without Mr. Sickles' knowledge and after my being told not to invite him to do so, and against Mr. Sickles' repeated request.

" 'Teresa Bagioli

" 'This is a true statement written by myself without any inducement held out by Mr. Sickles of forgiveness or reward, and without any menace from him. This I have written with my bedroom door open and my maid and child in adjoining room, at half past eight o'clock in the evening. Miss Ridgeley is in the house, within call.

" 'Teresa Bagioli' "

District Attorney Ould excitedly declared that this document could not possibly be included as evidence. It was a communication between husband and wife—parties who were excluded by law from testifying for or against each other. Brady replied with equal vigor that the statement was indeed admissible because it accounted for Sickles' state of mind at the time of the homicide. Back and forth wrangled Brady and Ould, each citing cases to support his contention, until the court adjourned for the day.

If Judge Crawford had his doubts about the relevance of Teresa Bagioli Sickles' confession, the Congressman and his attorneys did not. They proceeded to release it to the press, where it promptly made front pages around the world. Family, friends, and acquaintances of the lovely Teresa must have shuddered with disbelief, not only at the content of the confession but at the husband who could use it so ruthlessly. Sickles had been an intimate friend of Teresa's father, a noted New York opera impresario, and of her grandfather as well. He had known her from infancy, and had persuaded her, over considerable protests from her family, to abandon her convent education and marry him when she was only sixteen.

J. M. Carlisle opened the proceedings on the next day of the trial with a long, passionate speech against admitting the confession. Did the paper tend to show that the act committed the day after it was written was either justifiable homicide or manslaughter? he cried. It did not, unless His Honor held to the doctrine laid down by the other side—that no amount of time was sufficient to cool down the mind of a man under such provocation, and render him observant of the law of God and man. Was it evidence to show the prisoner's insanity? He would like to see what expert would declare "that such a declaration as this would tend to produce insanity in all or in a majority of cases. It would depend upon the moral and intellectual condition of the person."

Now Carlisle revealed for the first time his real role in the trial. If Ould, who held his job at the pleasure of the President, was afraid to strike at Buchanan's friend, Carlisle had no such inhibitions. There were, he said, two classes of men who could resist the insanity such a confession might cause. One was the convinced Christian, who would on his knees "pour out his supplication to Him who alone can bind up the broken heart." Then there was the second, "safe, quite safe from insanity, from such a blow as that— the confirmed adulterer, the open, shameless profligate— the man nurtured in brothels, the man breathing all his life the atmosphere of adultery and seduction . . . Now, to offer evidence of the fact of the adultery with the prisoner's wife as the ground to impute to him insanity, necessarily opens inquiry of the sort I have indicated. . . ."

This threat to explore the less than sanctified bypaths of Sickles' love life might have made some attorneys blanch. But it only seemed to make Sickles' triumvirate, especially Edwin Stanton, press on with even fiercer determination to get every last ugly fact of Key's adultery into the record. Perhaps they were influenced by Carlisle's inability to reach the jury's emotions, for all his rhetoric. "Nervous of manner yet cold of heart," as one eyewitness described him, Carlisle was a little too smooth for the role he had assigned himself.

Judge Crawford, after a recess, ruled Teresa's confession inadmissible because it would destroy before the law the "confidential identity" of the husband and wife. Unruffled by this ruling—a technicality that did nothing to erase the impact of the confession on the emotions of the jury— the defense summoned various witnesses. Bridget Duffy proceeded to describe Sickles' agitation on Sunday morning: how she saw him "come into the room crying aloud, his hands tearing his hair and in a state of distraction." More important was her description of Key's appearance in Lafayette Park, waving his handkerchief in a slow rotary motion. She told how the Sickles greyhound, Dandy, rushed out and fawned on Key, who ignored him. Sickles' good friend, George B. Wooldridge, confirmed these details. But when Brady attempted to lead Wooldridge into a discussion of what he had discovered about Key and Mrs. Sickles in his detective work the day before the killing, the prosecution once more objected.

This was too much for Stanton, who seized the center of the stage with a scathing attack on the prosecution's tactics thus far. He condemned Ould and Carlisle for their "thirst for blood" and begged the judge not to exclude evidence "in order that vengeance might obtain the blood of this prisoner." At this Ould leaped to his feet crying that it was sheer malice on Stanton's part to accuse a public prosecutor of being actuated by a thirst for blood. He vowed he would let his conduct in the case stand before the court and the world "in contrast with the disreputable rant" that Stanton had exhibited. Obviously, he declared, Stanton had been assigned the role of "the bully and the bruiser." Ignoring a mutter of protest that rose from the audience, Ould insisted he would stand by his oath and continue to call Sickles' deed murder, no matter what the defense called it.

Stanton met the District Attorney head on. He insisted that under the law Ould was defending, his client would be led to the gallows "by those who are malignantly seeking for his blood." He added that he did not have the honor of Ould's acquaintance "and after his language just uttered, [did] not desire it." This produced an uproar of approval in the courtroom, with much shouting and stamping of feet. It required considerable effort by the district marshal and his assisting officers to restore order.

In jail, the warden let Sickles stay in his own quarters instead of a cell; there he kept his dog and received guests.

Robert Ould, chief prosecutor

"Of course it is true that there are exasperations, and extenuations, and anger that conquers the will and the conscience, and strikes in an almost unconscious fury. But *ought* it to do so? Ought a man to be negatively praised for losing his moral control? Do we justify an engineer for not bridging precisely the worst abyss of all? The moral sense of every man is given him . . . for the trials that tear at his heart-roots. That sense may be overborne, and the man commit a crime as black as the one that exasperates him; but he is then not a man to be pitied as if he were a victim—he is to be pitied as a criminal. He may have more excuse than the seducer. But because the seduction of a woman is a crime, the willful murder of the seducer does not cease to be a crime also.

"And . . . remember . . . the real victim of the tragedy . . . a wayward girl fascinated to her ruin. If you hasten to pardon crime to him who sins through hate —will you deny forgiveness to her who falls through love: Tenderly, tenderly, pious souls!

"Owning her weakness,
Her evil behavior;
But leaving with meekness
Her sins to her Saviour."
—*Harper's Weekly,* March 12, 1859, p. 163

These pyrotechnics may have impressed the jury, but they got Stanton nowhere with Judge Crawford, who ruled that Wooldridge's communication to Sickles about Teresa's adultery was also inadmissible as evidence. This made little practical difference to the defense counsels, who had plenty of other ways to exploit the juicier aspects of the case. Witnesses testified to seeing Key waving his handkerchief in Lafayette Park for the better part of two hours— suggesting that he was one of the most indiscreet adulterers in history. Other witnesses recounted efforts made by Key's relatives and friends to padlock the house on 15th Street and remove any damaging evidence. Next came Nancy Brown, wife of President Buchanan's Negro gardener, who said that she lived on 15th Street and knew Key well by sight: "I saw him on the Wednesday before he was shot."

"Where did you see him?"

"I saw him going into a house on 15th Street . . ."

Carlisle leaped to his feet in a vain attempt to suppress the answer. Desperately he cried out that once more "they were sliding along in the direction of giving evidence of adultery." For once and for all he demanded that Judge Crawford rule on whether any evidence of this past adultery could be rightfully admitted. He declared that Judge Crawford was being given a chance to establish a "new era in the administration of justice in cases of homicide." In a long résumé of the defense's intentions as gleaned from the evidence presented thus far, Carlisle decried the tactic of painting the murdered Key and Sickles' wife in the blackest possible hues in order to justify the Congressman's crime. The whole concept of civilized law was at stake here, Carlisle insisted. Adultery was a crime under the laws of the District. Sickles had a legal recourse, as Judge Crawford would be the first to admit, since he himself had tried several cases of adultery in this very court.

Carlisle spoke for almost an hour. Brady then coolly rose and exploded his plea with a single question. "Was the case of adultery to which you refer as being tried here an indictment under the statute?"

"Yes, under the statute of Maryland."

Now Sickles' use of local attorneys paid off. Mr. Magruder made the point that under the statute of Maryland the punishment for that crime was a fine of a hundred pounds of tobacco.

"Then the only satisfaction an injured husband could have," snorted Brady, "would be a chew of tobacco." The courtroom exploded with laughter.

Despite the fact that more court time already had been devoted to Key's act of adultery than to Sickles' act of homicide, Judge Crawford had not yet explicitly conceded that evidence of the adultery had any legal bearing on the trial. For days this point was wrangled over by the lawyers on both sides, while the Judge, obviously harassed and puzzled, pondered the question. Then, on the thirteenth day of the trial—Monday, April 18—he announced his decision. Sickles' cry about his defiled bed, at the moment of the shooting, intoned His Honor, was reason enough to admit the evidence of adultery as an "explanation." There was, declared Felix G. Fontaine, who published a transcript of the trial, "a perceptible though silent expression of satisfaction" in the audience when Judge Crawford pronounced this decision.

Jubilation undoubtedly reigned at the defense table. Witness after witness now paraded to the stand, giving vivid details of Key and Teresa Sickles scuttling down 15th Street to their love nest in the Negro slum known as Dark Town, or trysting in the Sickles study when the Congressman was away. Nancy Brown told how Key would hang a string from the upstairs shutters of the 15th Street house to signal to his mistress that the coast was clear. Everyone on the entire block, and every servant in Sickles' house, seemed to know what was going on, but not Dan Sickles.

By now it was hard to tell whether Sickles was on trial for murder or Key for adultery. But there was still one flaw in the case for the defense. Sickles had rushed into the street, loaded with lethal artillery, and shot down an apparently unarmed man. The next witness was designed

"An injured husband has but three ways of meeting the injury. He may laugh at it, or he may challenge his enemy; this is the French method. The first recourse affords but little consolation, and requires unusual philosophy; the second may superadd physical to moral injury. He may sue the adulterer for damages. This is the English plan. It involves patience, delay, exposure, disgrace.... Finally, the injured husband may take the life of him who has injured him. This is the American system.... Terrible as homicide is, this method must, on the whole, be admitted to be the most effectual, the wisest, and the most natural revenge....

"There can be no excuse for the adulterer. He commits a three-fold crime: a crime against the woman whom he misleads, a crime against the man whom he dishonors, a crime against society which he disorganizes.... In these latter days experience proves that in all such cases society will justify the infliction of the last penalty by the husband. Whatever may have been the character of Mr. Sickles, there is not a jury in the United States or in Europe which would convict him even of manslaughter. In the face of so decided a public sentiment, is it worth while to argue further on the question?"
—*Harper's Weekly*, March 12, 1859, p. 162

James Brady, for the defense

to remove this last potential element of sympathy for Key. A contractor named Albert A. Megaffey declared he was "tolerably intimate" with Key, and proceeded to recount a series of conversations he had had with the late district attorney about his attentions to Mrs. Sickles. Megaffey had warned Key that he might get into danger or difficulty about the matter. In reply, he said, Key laid his hand on the left breast of his coat and declared, "I am prepared for any emergency."

A new uproar ensued. Ould and Carlisle, almost wild with exasperation, cried that these conversations, the last of which took place twelve days before the murder, surely had no bearing on the case. They certainly did not tend to prove that Key was armed on the day of his death, or even that Sickles thought he was armed, since Mr. Megaffey never communicated anything about the conversation to the Congressman. The Judge emphatically agreed with the prosecution, and barred Megaffey's testimony. But the defense had scored another victory with the jury, who now saw at least the possibility that Key had had a gun in his pocket.

Throughout the long trial, Dan Sickles had sat silent in his prisoner's pen. It must have been a difficult feat for a man who found it almost impossible to ignore a fight. Equally tormenting must have been the sniggering testimony of his own servants recalling how they had referred to Key and Mrs. Sickles as Disgrace and Disgust and opining that more than once the clandestine couple "wasn't at no good work." Yet Sickles lost his composure only once, when Robert Walker, former senator from Mississippi and one-time Secretary of the Treasury, told of rushing to the Sickles house after the shooting and finding the Congressman on the edge of insanity. Walker described "unnatural and unearthly sounds. The most remarkable I ever heard —something like a scream interrupted by violent sobbing."

At this testimony Dan Sickles collapsed, and his sobs were audible throughout the courtroom. Judge Crawford ordered a recess, and the prisoner's friends, followed by his weeping father, helped him outside, where he regained his self-control. One reason for this breakdown, unknown at the time, may have been a correspondence that Sickles had opened with his wife while he was in jail awaiting trial. In the early days of the trial she had written him:

"You say that any object you have loved remains dear to you. Do I now stand upon a footing with the other women I know you have loved? I have long felt like asking you what your love affairs have been—love of the heart, or love of their superior qualities such as you have often informed me I did not possess, or attraction of face and form, or an infatuation? If during the first years we were married my good conduct did not keep you true to me, can I suppose for a moment the last year has? *Ask your own heart who sinned first, and then tell me, if you will.*"

J. M. Carlisle, bitter over his defeat on the adultery issue, no doubt would have given much for a copy of that letter. He was now more than ever determined to examine Sickles' amatory past. But he held his fire, meanwhile chipping away at the defense contention that Sickles was insane. Here once more District Attorney Ould was undone by the aggressive defense. When Ould asked Francis Doyle, who had been present when the dying Key was carried into the Cosmos Club, to give the court a description of Sickles' demeanor, Stanton protested, making the remarkable declaration that the burden of proof was on the *prosecution* to show that Sickles "was a person of sound memory and discretion at the time the act was committed." This produced more than a few splutterings from Judge Crawford, who hastened to declare that every man "is presumed to be sane till the contrary is proved; that is the normal condition of the human race, I hope."

Now, though his gentlemanly soul no doubt recoiled from it, Carlisle resolved to use his last weapon. In court was the proprietor of a Baltimore hotel with its register under his arm. He was prepared to show that on a date not too long before the day of the murder, Sickles had

.... I have been in a house in 15ᵗʰ St. with Mr. Key; how many times I don't know...

Teresa Sickles' written confession made this nondescript house in a Negro section of Washington a notorious landmark.

visited that hotel with a lady who signed herself as Mrs. Sickles, though her handwriting clearly proved she was not.

But chunky Robert Ould, though he lacked fire, was a solid, well-trained lawyer; he knew that such evidence could not be introduced by the prosecution with the same reckless effrontery displayed by the defense. If Messrs. Graham, Brady, and Stanton objected to it as irrelevant and the judge sustained them, they would immediately move for a mistrial on the grounds that the jury's mind had been fatally prejudiced against the prisoner.

Thus Ould did the only thing a sensible prosecutor could do in such a situation. He submitted the incriminating ledger to the attorneys for the defense, before airing it publicly. Inevitably they objected, and the matter was referred to Judge Crawford for decision. *Sotto voce,* both sides argued before His Honor for several minutes. Then, wizened cheeks twitching, Crawford proceeded to declare: "For very obvious reasons the court will do no more than merely state his opinion on this point, and that opinion is that the evidence is *not* admissible."

There was nothing left now but the summation. In a long, passionate speech for the defense, Stanton covered much of the ground Graham had discussed in his opening oration. But his sarcasm was more biting, his denunciation of Key more intense. Again and again the courtroom burst into applause as he scored another sulphurous point against the adulterer whose deeds surpassed "all that has ever been written of cold, villainous, remorseless lust." Beside this Old Testament fury, the District Attorney seemed pale indeed, citing the New Testament example of Christ, who forgave the adulteress. Didn't the same argument, he pleaded, apply to Philip Barton Key? Then Ould touched, at the very last moment, on a theme that he might well have used effectively earlier: If Philip Barton Key were alive, he, and he alone, might be able to produce evidence that might show that he was more seduced than seducer; that he had yielded to "temptations repeated and continued until those higher moral bulwarks that should have supported his character gave way beneath repeated shocks."

James T. Brady tartly recalled a passage of previous

Mr. Fleming has written many books and articles; this is the second of a series on great American trials which he is doing for AMERICAN HERITAGE. *The next, on the trial of John Brown, will appear in an early issue.*

For further reading: Sickles the Incredible, *by W. A. Swanberg (Scribner's, 1956).*

testimony that had quoted Key himself to the effect that Mrs. Sickles was a mere child, and that he stood in parental relation to her.

Ould let the topic drop without another word.

The Judge's instructions to the jury caused the defense only mild alarm. He followed the traditional legal rule of thumb which held that the husband who killed an adulterer a day or even a half day after his act, rather than *flagrante delicto,* committed murder. But Crawford agreed with the main defense contention: "If the jury have any doubt as to the case, either in reference to the homicide or the question of sanity, Mr. Sickles should be acquitted."

Judge Crawford finished his instructions to the jury early on the twentieth and last day of the trial. Brady now rose for the defense and suggested that the case be submitted to the jury without additional summing up on either side. Robert Ould half rose from his seat and wearily concurred.

Friends crowded around the prisoner in his pen, assuring him it would all be over in five minutes. But the clock crept past the half-hour mark, and then the hour, with no sign of a forgiving jury. At the defense table, James Brady's face was by now pale and solemn. In the jury room, the wrangling was feverish. Only seven were for acquittal at the first vote; three were in doubt; two were firmly opposed. But the majority first convinced the doubters, and then went to work on the opposition. Both were intensely religious men, who obviously agreed with Ould's closing arguments. Finally one, a stern Presbyterian, yielded. The last suddenly broke away from the group, knelt in a corner, and prayed silently for guidance. Then he returned and said: "I have my answer. Let the prisoner go free."

When Foreman Arnold announced the verdict, the courtroom went berserk. Brady burst into tears. Edwin Stanton did a highly uncharacteristic jig and called for three cheers. Other friends rushed up to kiss and embrace Sickles. Outside in the streets an enormous crowd hurrahed wildly and tried to unhorse Sickles' carriage so they could pull him through the capital like a conquering hero.

Jury verdicts do not constitute precedents, in the American legal system, and no lawyer has ever urged a judge to remind a jury of Dan Sickles' acquittal. Strictly speaking the jury ruled against the proper interpretation of the law, and the law remained unchanged. Nevertheless, in years to come journalists frequently referred to the case as justifying the "unwritten law." Actually, as we have seen, Sickles' lawyers were too shrewd to rest their argument on a single plea, and utilized every possible argument from temporary insanity to justifiable homicide to save their client. The case did illustrate the wisdom of an adage at least as old as the jury system and as new as the latest murder trial in yesterday's headlines: when you're on trial for your life, hire the very best legal talent you can afford.

Later that year Sickles, in a gesture of generosity, took Teresa back as his wife—an act for which he was bitterly denounced by the same people who had acclaimed his "defense" of his bed and home. She never appeared with him in society again, however, and died eight years later, a wasted ghost of the young hostess who had charmed Washington. As for Congressman Sickles, another kind of gunfire along the Potomac soon converted him into a national hero of sorts. Wangling himself a major-generalship, he served courageously on a dozen Civil War battlefields. But even here, his genius for personal imbroglios made him a controversial figure. One school of thought, led by Sickles, argued that Dan really won the Battle of Gettysburg by taking a highly exposed position in a wheat field and orchard. Other military thinkers accused him of almost losing it, because his corps was torn to bits by a three-sided Southern assault, leaving a huge hole in the Union line. (Sickles lost a leg to a Confederate cannon ball.) But Dan insisted that the whole battle had gone exactly according to his plan: he had taken the position with clear foreknowledge that he was inviting the Southern onrush, which his brave boys blunted, enabling a reinforced second line to stop the Rebs for good. His powers of persuasion later inspired no less than James Longstreet, the Confederate general who had delivered the assault, to agree with him.

After the war Sickles served as minister to Spain under Grant, won himself a third term in Congress in 1893, and ended his days with another scandal—the New York State Monuments Commission, of which he was chairman, suddenly discovered it was some twenty-eight thousand dollars short of funds. Friends and relatives made up the difference, and Dan died at ninety-five, still one jump ahead of the bailiffs. Well into his eighties he continued to chase the girls, listing among his conquests ex-Queen Isabella of Spain—who, however, was easily his match in promiscuity. His second wife, whom he married in Spain, left him (after bearing two children) because he was habitually unfaithful. Perhaps George Templeton Strong summed up Daniel E. Sickles best when he wrote in his diary, "One might as well try to spoil a rotten egg as to damage Dan's character."

Mr. Key, after Mr. Sickles had taken "a husband's revenge"

that the boats would keep coming back until all were off the ship.

For the crew, there were the final duties—the sort they had practiced for months at drill but never really expected to have to perform. Dr. Grazier made ready to abandon his first-aid post set up on the steel gratings over the engine room. During a lull in the bombings, he and an assistant had searched through the demolished sick bay on the upper deck. There they had salvaged all health records and as many medical dressings, drugs, and antiseptics as could be crammed into a sturdy pillow case. Grazier saw all his wounded loaded into the boats, then climbed down himself.

Ensign Biwerse made one last trip to the radio room. He grabbed what confidential publications he could find and tossed them over the side. Weighted lead jackets binding the code books made them sink immediately. Then Biwerse and a crew of sailors began to load emergency rations, clothes, and blankets into one of the boats. Their inventory ranged from one of the Lewis machine guns with ammunition to a bushel basket of fresh eggs. The eggs were to come in much handier than the gun.

Lieutenant Geist ordered steam released from the single boiler that had been in use. When the cold water of the Yangtze hit it, he did not want it to explode. Then he headed for the wardroom, where the ship's money was kept—vouchers and about $40,-000 in cash. But the safe doors were sprung shut by the bombs. Water was beginning to come into the wardroom rapidly, and it was at deck level; that meant the *Panay*'s hull was almost awash. Geist had to back out empty-handed.

At 3:05 P.M., the last man stepped off the ship. With flags flying, the *Panay* was abandoned—the first ship of the U.S. Navy ever lost to enemy aircraft and, in a sense, the first naval casualty of World War II.

By the time the boats started toward shore the bombing runs had stopped, but Japanese planes still wheeled overhead and swooped down over the survivors. More than once their machine guns cut loose, and the boats were struck several times. Two seamen already wounded in the bombing attack were hit again. "The strafing," said London *Times* correspondent Colin McDonald, who was in the boat with these wounded seamen, "seemed like the end of a deliberate, systematic attempt to destroy the gunboat and all on board." McDonald tore up handkerchiefs and rags to stuff in the bullet holes in the boat, and then started to bail rapidly with the only thing available—a helmet.

Ashore, Storekeeper First Class Charles L. Ensminger of Ocean Beach, California, was dying. So was Sandro Sandri, an Italian journalist known as "the Floyd Gibbons of Italy," who was stretched out in the reeds with excruciatingly painful stomach wounds. Luigi Barzini, his Italian companion, could only comfort him with an occasional cigarette and a word from time to time.

When the last boat trip had been made to shore, Commander Hughes propped himself up in his basket stretcher in the reeds to take stock of the situation. It was not encouraging. All his line officers except one had been wounded in some degree; the "unharmed" survivor was Ensign Biwerse, and he was groggy from shock. Hughes's party contained fifteen stretcher cases. A dozen or so others could walk with their wounds or were suffering from concussion. The ranking line officer of either service still on his feet was Army Captain Roberts. Hughes asked him to take active leadership.

If, as it appeared, the Japanese were out to finish off all the survivors, the best plan would be to move away from the immediate location as quickly as possible. J. Hall Paxton, the second secretary of the Nanking embassy and a veteran in the China service, was to go ahead on foot to try to get word of the attack back to Ambassador Nelson T. Johnson at Hankow.

Out on the river the *Panay* was getting a humiliating *coup de grâce*. From downstream two Japanese army motorboats had moved up abeam of the ship and were firing aimlessly into the slowly settling superstructure. When several short bursts had evoked no return fire or other sign of life aboard the sinking gunboat, the launches closed in. The Japanese soldiers boarded the *Panay*, made a perfunctory search while the Stars and Stripes still cracked out over their heads in the chill December wind—and then, satisfied that she was abandoned and going down, the soldiers left and headed upriver again. A short time later there was the sound of two muffled explosions from within the ship. At 3:54 P.M., as the men on the shore doffed their caps, the *Panay* slid under, bow first. Both newsreel cameraman Norman Alley and Norman Soong, a Hawaiian-born American of Chinese ancestry who was a photographer for the *New York Times,* recorded the final plunge. The two men had taken valuable photographic evidence that would prove the attacking Japanese planes had been low enough, on more than one approach, for good identification.

Several men remembered later the sudden lonely feeling of being stranded. They were not at all sure anyone knew of their difficulty. And even if there had been no other problems, they were in a miserable spot. The riverbank where the Americans had first landed was little more than the muddy edge of a swamp of high reeds. The footing was precarious—freezing but not frozen. There had been a good bit of splashing around, slipping and sliding in the icy swamp water and the mud of the bank, trying to find some place on which to lay the wounded—ground that was both out of the water and still hidden from further Japanese attack.

A few minutes after the *Panay* finally settled below the surface of the river, Japanese planes came again. A pair of them circled low over the swamp for what seemed to the hiding Americans an interminable time. But the survivors weren't spotted in the ten-foot-high reeds. The aircraft departed into the growing dusk after methodically dropping their bombs on two of the Standard Oil tankers which had been beached on the south bank of the river after the initial bombing. Both ships blazed up; the screams of the Chinese crewmen were audible across the mile of water. Hardly had the sounds of the airplane engines faded when a small Japanese patrol boat appeared and passed slowly along the shore as if it, too, were looking for survivors. The Americans stayed low, for they were defenseless: The one machine gun Biwerse had brought ashore had already been dismantled and tossed into the swamp to prevent its capture; the men were determined there would be no trophies for the victors.

As soon as it was dark the survivors moved out of the tall reeds and assembled again at the river's edge alongside an abandoned motor launch. Many of the men were dressed only in the light clothes they had been wearing below decks in the early afternoon when the attack had begun. Some were without shoes. One sailor had been taking a bath when the first bomb dropped, and had manned one of the Lewis guns clad only in life jacket, helmet, and righteous indignation. On shore, he had to piece together an outfit through the largess of several better-dressed survivors.

The wounded—a few on stretchers brought off from the ship, but most of them slung painfully and awkwardly in ship's blankets—were placed aboard the launch. Then the whole party moved on along the river toward the nearby hamlet of Ho Chan, their way lighted by the blaze from the tankers. From time to time explosions sent burning fragments and red-hot chunks of metal sizzling down into the river.

At the hamlet, the survivors were met by a small party of Chinese police who had witnessed the bombing. Additional stretchers were improvised from fence rails, bed springs, and the doors of farm buildings. Some frightened coolies were recruited to help with

"Sank one of his own, too," observed a cartoonist for the Milwaukee Journal, *commenting on the sinking of the* Panay.

the wounded. About 9 P.M., after a meager meal of Biwerse's eggs and some tea, the journey was begun again—to Hohsien, a little walled village about seven miles from the scene of the sinking. "Eventually," wrote correspondent McDonald, "the gate of Hohsien was reached about midnight, but it was nearly dawn before the last of the wounded was carried into a derelict hospital on a hill above the shrouded town where Dr. Grazier again worked without rest to relieve their sufferings." About three thirty Monday morning, in that miserable, unheated little hospital, Storekeeper Ensminger died of his wounds. Sandri died a little past noon.

Three times on Monday, Japanese planes swooped low over Hohsien—seeming to dive particularly at the flimsy, straw-roofed hospital. The Japanese claimed later that these were rescue planes trying to spot the *Panay* shore party and give assistance, but in the light of preceding events, attack seemed a more likely motive. It was decided that as soon as darkness came on Monday night, the *Panay*'s people should move on again to Hanshan, the first town of any size outside the probable area of hostilities. First, however, the bodies of Ensminger and Sandri were prepared for burial. The coffins would have to be left behind, to be picked up later by other gunboats. The able-bodied officers and men were drawn up for a final salute to their dead shipmate. Local magistrate Wang Tien Chih, a Syracuse University graduate, placed an American flag over the sailor's body. Then the wounded and the walking embarked in a tiny convoy of eight open junks for another trip through the freezing night by canal to Hanshan, twenty-five miles to the northwest.

At daylight Tuesday they reached this refuge to find that Paxton, the embassy man who had gone on ahead of the main party, had succeeded in getting a message through. An American missionary, Dr. C. A. Birch, had arrived from his station 130 miles away with a car full of medical supplies.

Early Tuesday afternoon, while the survivors at Hanshan were enjoying their first real meal since Sunday dinner, the British gunboat Bee arrived in Hohsien to pick them up. U.S.S. Oahu was close behind, with Ladybird, another British gunboat.* The Americans retraced their path to the river.

On Wednesday morning, December 15, in a dense fog, the main body of Panay survivors finally reached the clean, warm sanctuary of the three gunboats, where hot food, medical attention, and contact with a seriously alarmed outside world waited for them. With them came four rough wooden coffins containing the bodies of Ensminger, Sandri, C. H. Carlson, captain of one of the Standard Oil tankers, and the Chinese quartermaster of another tanker.

U.S.S. Oahu, Lieutenant Commander J. M. Sheehan commanding, had joined the Bee off Hohsien at about the same time that the first survivors arrived back at the town. Hardly had the Oahu anchored when a boat came over from one of the Japanese destroyers also standing by. It carried two Japanese naval surgeons and a Japanese hospital corpsman. They requested Sheehan's permission to board, saying that they had been sent to assist with the wounded. The American officer at first declined their aid, but they were very insistent. "And rather than cause unpleasantness," Sheehan reported, "I let them stay and sent them to the sick bay to await the arrival of the wounded." A short time after the first survivors started coming aboard, Sheehan looked in to see his own doctor at work, with the Japanese close at the American's side, "ostensibly to assist, but actually they were taking notes of injuries and conditions of men."

* The British boats had been attacked by the Japanese, too. On the same afternoon the Panay was bombed, Bee and Ladybird had been shelled by Japanese artillery as they cruised about thirty miles upstream. The gunboats returned the fire, suffering light casualties—one killed, four wounded. Two other British craft, Cricket and Scarab, had been bombed near Nanking by one of the squadrons that had hit the Panay a few hours earlier.

It was noon Wednesday before the fog at Hohsien lifted—and 1 P.M. before the somber procession started back downriver for Shanghai. A Japanese torpedo boat was in the lead. Then came U.S.S. Oahu with the survivors. H.M.S. Ladybird, carrying the coffins of Ensminger and Sandri, and another Japanese vessel brought up the rear. The Bee had gone on ahead. Colors on all ships were at half mast.

On Friday at 4:30 P.M. in the gathering winter dusk, the Oahu steamed slowly around the bend below Shanghai's bund and eased alongside the Augusta. In a wireless story to the New York Times from Shanghai, correspondent Hallett Abend described the moving scene that millions of Americans would see later on their newsreel screens:

When the Oahu was first sighted, a curious murmur of suppressed excitement was felt the whole length of the 10,000-ton cruiser, whose decks were crowded with officers, sailors, marines, and a few civilians. It was not a manifestation of relief or enthusiasm when the Oahu made fast alongside the Augusta. Instead, those aboard the flagship stood in oppressed silence when they saw the survivors on the Oahu decks, whose faces in most cases were drawn and lined, many suffering obviously from shell shock; others had their arms in slings, while others wore conspicuous bandages.

A few hands were raised in salutes and greetings, and a few almost-hushed salutations were exchanged across the narrowing waters as the ships drew together while daylight faded rapidly. A hastily improvised gangway, of unplaned and unpainted lumber, was shoved from Augusta's deck onto Oahu's top deck, and a few of Augusta's officers boarded the rescue ship. Then came a long wait, after which Augusta sailors carried empty stretchers aboard the Oahu, while blue-uniformed marines guarded the gangway and a majority of Augusta's officers stood silent, waiting, in a semicircle. Admiral Harry E. Yarnell, Commander-in-Chief of the United States Asiatic Fleet, sat grim-faced in his quarters awaiting oral reports of surviving officers on the Panay, many of whom were grievously wounded.

For the officers and men of the Panay and for their surviving civilian passengers, the "incident" was almost over. Some would be in and out of hospitals for months before they were able to return to duty. Some would be invalided out of service. One of them, Coxswain Edgar W. G. Hulsebus, would die in a Shanghai hospital, bringing the Panay's death toll to three.

And there was still a court of inquiry to be closed. It had commenced aboard the Augusta on December 16, and moved to the hospital bedsides of assorted survivors; it concluded two days before Christmas. The court found, in summary, that everything possible had been done first to defend the ship and then to try to save her when she was mortally struck. There were several recommendations. The first asked that a board be convened to award decorations. The second concerned salvage: Since some of the ship's confidential publications had gone down with her, their security had to be considered compromised until salvage could be accomplished—or declared impossible. The third recommendation urged that "the inadequacy of the antiaircraft defense for naval ships be given immediate consideration by the Navy Department." Two months later, reviewing the findings of the court, the Navy's Bureau of Ordnance replied starchily that "with reference to the Court's third recommendation . . . antiaircraft defense of naval ships is under continual consideration and study by this bureau."

There were several bills to be rendered, too. Standard Oil had put its losses at $1,594,435.99. The Navy asked for $1,211,355.01. Of this amount, $607,000 represented claims for the death of Ensminger and Hulsebus, and for personal injuries to the fifty-seven officers and men who suffered from wounds, shock, or exposure. When submitting the Navy bill to the State Department for transmission to the Japanese, Secretary of the Navy Claude A. Swanson emphasized that even this substantial amount did not include damages for injuries to civilians, or to State Department or War Department personnel on board.

The initial Japanese reaction to the news of the sinking was one of shock and regret for what was officially declared a tragic case of mistaken identity. A Japanese communiqué pledged immediate action in identifying the military units responsible.

Vice Admiral Kiyoshi Hasegawa, commander of all Japanese naval forces in Chinese waters, immediately called on Admiral Yarnell to express his regrets. The meeting was icy, even though Hasegawa promised Yarnell he would accept "the fullest personal responsibility." In the Japanese military code, that could mean resignation or even hara-kiri. Hasegawa was in a tight spot. The Japanese Navy had recently bragged that it had sunk every Chinese warship on the river. But if that were true, why did Japanese pilots mistake the floating Panay for the sunken enemy?

In Washington on Monday, December 13, Secretary of State Cordell Hull delivered to Japanese Ambassador Hirosi Saito a memo of protest demanding full apology and compensations for the sinking.

In Tokyo, a delegation of high-school girls representing 500 students at the White Lily School left a donation at the Japanese Navy Ministry for Panay survivors. At the Japanese Foreign Office, two Japanese boys, eleven and fifteen, called to leave a donation of two dollars for the Americans. U.S. Ambassador Joseph Grew was deluged by apologies and expressions of sympathy from representatives of all classes, from high officials to school children. In several cases his wife was privately called upon by the wives of highly placed Japanese who felt they could not show their regret publicly. The conduct of the people was moving, but Grew feared the United States was in a remember-the-Maine mood; he was already making plans for the evacuation of the embassy should it be ordered.

The Emperor was said to have had his naval ministers on the carpet, rubbing their noses deep in the pile. The Japanese government insisted that since the outbreak of hostilities in China in July, it had faithfully tried to prevent what had just happened. During that time, the government said, a number of fliers had been punished and some sent back to Japan in disgrace for "reckless flying." More immediately to the point, the government announced that Rear Admiral Keizo Mutsunami, commander of the Japanese Naval Air Force in China, had been dismissed and ordered to return to Japan immediately. Mutsunami had seemed sure of a bright future: he had once been skipper of the big carrier Kaga, which was to take part four years later in the Pearl Harbor attack, and only recently had been made a rear admiral. Virtually his whole career had been with the naval air forces. Now it was presumably over.

By Friday, December 17, the day the survivors reached Shanghai, many U.S. papers reported for the first time the final ignominious machine-gunning of the Panay by Japanese army craft before she sank. The story did not appear in Japanese papers; the Foreign Office in Tokyo immediately reported to Washington that the reply to the earlier American protest would have to be delayed still further while it looked into this new charge. Meantime, despite Japanese investigations and apologies, American indignation was growing.

On Monday, December 20, the Japanese admitted for the first time that indeed there had been from close range, where no mistake of identity should have been involved, a machine-gun attack against the sinking gunboat by Japanese army launches. New York

U.S. GUNBOAT SUNK BY JAPANESE BOMBS; 1 DEAD AND 15 HURT; 54 SAVED, 18 MISSING; BRITISH WARSHIP HIT, SEAMAN DEAD

New York Times, DECEMBER 13, 1937

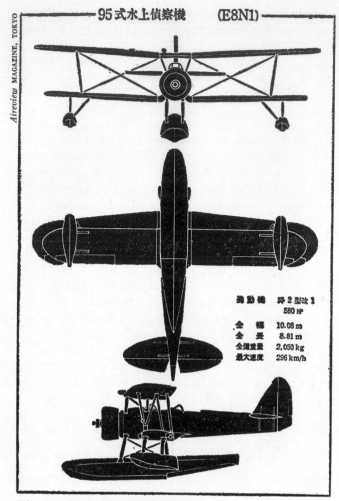

95式水上偵察機　　（E8N1）

弾動機　　　丹2型改1
　　　　　　580 HP

全　幅　　　10.08 m
全　長　　　8.81 m
全備重量　　2,050 kg
最大速度　　296 km/h

The attack on the Panay *was made by Japanese airplanes whose design copied, to a large extent, the U.S. Corsair.*

Times correspondent Abend reported in an exclusive story that the machine-gunning was done on the personal command of one Colonel Kingoro Hashimoto. It was also suggested that in some unexplained way the Japanese navy fliers who made the initial attack might have been temporarily under Hashimoto's command. The Colonel's responsibility for the order was no secret in the Japanese Army, Abend wrote. Hashimoto was still in the field, presumably unavailable and obviously unchastised.

Hashimoto's background reveals some reasons why his superior officers may have hesitated to discipline him. He had been one of the leaders in a coup the year before, when a clique of about 1,000 young army officers had seized the government building and communications centers in Tokyo and killed Premier Keisuke Okada and three cabinet members. The plotters had placed the capital under martial law and had staged a reign of terror for several days until subdued by loyal government troops. Hashimoto obviously must have had valuable political protection, for he had simply

been relieved of duty. He had then formed the Greater Japan Youth Party, and guided it in general trouble-making until he had been recalled to duty and sent to China in the fall of 1937. Now, apparently, his political protection was still good.

The machine-gunning of the ship and Hashimoto's role in the incident were now receiving more attention in the American press than the bombing itself. The Japanese papers still carried no mention of the attack by the army launches. But to Americans, the machine-gun outrage seemed to indicate clearly that the whole incident had been carefully planned from beginning to end by the anti-Western faction in the Japanese Army in order to humiliate the United States.

It was Christmas Eve in Washington—a "masterful" piece of timing, Ambassador Grew called it—when the official Japanese answer finally came. With it came a strange feeling of anticlimax—and relief. The reply was a complete apology. All the particulars of the U.S. note had been met. The Japanese still maintained that the bombing was a colossal mistake, although an understandable one. While the *Panay*'s plan of movement had been properly filed with military authorities, erratic field communications between Japanese units had held up a proper passing of the word. The commander of the air squadron that sank the gunboat had not been notified of the *Panay*'s presence in that part of the river until 5:30 P.M.—an hour and a half after she had gone to the bottom. And in spite of the American photographs, which showed that the visibility had been fine, the Japanese claimed that "dense smoke" had so obscured the area that Japanese troops had also been bombed. At the time the Japanese had said that only fifteen planes had been involved in five attacks over about twenty minutes' time; later admissions raised the attacking force to twenty-four. The pilots stoutly denied that American flags had been seen at any time, even though they said they had dived as low as 900 feet to try to identify the vessels. The Japanese also reported that those responsible had been punished, but Colonel Hashimoto was not named or alluded to.

On April 22, 1938, the *Panay* incident was officially marked closed when the Japanese government presented the United States with a check for $2,214,007.36. It was tendered as "settlement in full" for destroying three large Standard Oil craft, for the loss of the *Panay*, for the deaths of one civilian captain and two Navy men, and for injuries suffered by seventy-four men on all the vessels.

But the men who had been bombed and machine-gunned didn't close the books so quickly, and neither did their country. Dr. Grazier and twenty-two enlisted men were recommended for the Navy Cross.

Special letters of commendation from the Secretary of the Navy went to Lieutenant Commander Hughes and two other crewmen, one of them Chinese-born. Another crewman of Chinese origin got the Bronze Star. Executive Officer Anders, who took over for his disabled skipper, and Captain Roberts, the embassy military attaché, each received a Distinguished Service Medal. The Navy further honored Army Captain Roberts with the Navy Cross for his "fortitude and heroism."

Only one of the four crack flight leaders who led the twenty-four Japanese planes on their attack against the *Panay* survived World War II. Commander Masatake Okumiya lived through four years of combat to see peace come again to Japan. In an article in an American naval journal in 1953, Okumiya wrote his account of the *Panay* sinking, still claiming that it had been a case of mistaken identity. He insisted that the command structure of the two services made it "impossible" for Army fire-eaters to have duped the Japanese Navy and ordered the attack. Okumiya did have a few barbs for his sister service. He criticized the Army—and particularly Colonel Hashimoto—because Army spokesmen had repeatedly aggravated the bad feeling that followed the sinking by not showing "common sense in regard to international matters, nor did they display good judgment, or even proper knowledge of military etiquette."

Colonel Hashimoto was recalled to Japan early in 1938 and put on inactive duty, but he was never disciplined otherwise. After Pearl Harbor, the official pose of displeasure was no longer necessary. On January 25, 1942—forty-nine days after the Hawaiian raid—Hashimoto was awarded the Kinshi Kinsho Medal for his "audacity" in ordering attacks on all ships in the Yangtze four years earlier. While the bombing of the *Panay* was not specified, the citation was general enough to cover it—without leaving the government open to the charge of having lied when it ignored Hashimoto's role four years earlier. Though still carrying the rank of colonel in 1942, he made his contribution during the war in the Japanese Diet and as a vigorous leader of the extremists and unofficial inner-circle government leaders who advocated Japanese control not only of East Asia, but of Australia, New Zealand, Madagascar, and India as well.

On April 29, 1946, the Colonel stood among the twenty-eight top Japanese leaders who were indicted for "plotting to rule the world." A staggering fifty-five counts of war crimes were arrayed against them. It was made clear in the indictment that the trials would involve charges of aggression even before the Japanese invasion of Manchuria in 1931. The trial had been in progress about three months when the *Panay* incident

was revived in court—over the strong protest of the defense lawyers. Hashimoto admitted that his artillery had shelled H.M.S. *Ladybird* on her way to aid the *Panay*'s survivors. That was as far as he would go. Almost a year passed before Hashimoto came back into the limelight again. This time he admitted to prosecutors his long-time role as a troublemaker; he conceded that he had been a member of a tightly organized group that had been behind attempts to control the Japanese government since 1931, and that he had long advocated bringing to an end British political control in the Orient—"by force if necessary." When the trial came to an end on November 12, 1948, Hashimoto was sentenced to life imprisonment.

On September 17, 1955—ten years and one day after he had given himself up to Allied authorities—the little colonel walked out of Tokyo's Sugamo Prison a free man, but with incurable cancer. He had been released "by agreement of the United States and seven other Allied powers." He and two other political prisoners emerged impeccably dressed in morning coats and striped trousers.

If Hashimoto had a secret—that he had been the man chosen to test Western toughness with an overt attack that might show whether or not the U.S. would risk war—two years later it died with him.

A year after the *Panay* was sunk, divers recovered her safe from the muddy waters of the Yangtze. More than $40,000 in cash and the vouchers and pay accounts were recovered intact. After their examination, John Geist, the *Panay*'s disbursing officer, then on duty in Manila, received the standard form letter from the Secretary of the Navy reporting that the money had been recovered, "your accounts are in order, and you may now resume your duties." Unless the Chinese Communists have high regard for old scrap or the resurrected relics of history, the *Panay*'s hull is still at the bottom of the river.

Geist and eleven other *Panay* survivors were at Pearl Harbor on December 7, 1941. As they saw the bombers with the red suns on their wingtips come diving down again there was an awful familiarity to it all.

But this time there would be no apologies.

Darby Perry has recently been appointed publisher of AMERICAN HERITAGE. *For this article he interviewed or corresponded with several* Panay *survivors and with Japanese pilots who participated in the attack. He is now at work on a book about the incident. The editors wish to thank Arthur F. Anders, the* Panay's *executive officer, for permission to photograph the blood-stained chart on which he wrote his orders (see page 41). Mr. Anders, now a retired commander living in California, has a son, Air Force Major William A. Anders, in the astronaut program. It is only one generation from gunboat times to the space age.*

READING, WRITING, AND HISTORY

By BRUCE CATTON

The Dreadful Noise

A man who tried to play the violin in public without studying the rules of music and the techniques of musicianship would of course need to have his head examined. (He would also need to be silenced, but that would come automatically.) Not even in this permissive age would anyone argue that the simple desire to produce pleasing sounds could make up for a total lack of craftsmanship, because it is so obvious that without craftsmanship the sounds would not be pleasing.

In other words, there are rules that have to be observed by anyone who wants to make music. These rules are rigid, the student has to work within their limits, and he cannot do it unless he knows what the rules are and what they require of him. He may be able to whistle a tune acceptably without this knowledge, but if he wants to go further he must prepare himself. The violin is a marvelously flexible and expressive instrument, but when it is badly handled it makes a dreadful noise.

What is true of the violin is also true of the English language. You can do almost anything you want to do with it if you know how to handle it, but there are rules to be observed. Some of them seem arbitrary, and learning to work with them can be a great deal of trouble, but to go ahead without even knowing what they are and why they exist is dangerous. In trying to produce persuasive prose, the writer is likely to commit an atrocity.

This to be sure would not be worth saying, except that so many educators nowadays are arguing that the rules no longer exist. If you can speak the language, we are told, you can write it: go ahead boldly with never a backward glance, and if you make a hash out of grammar and syntax nobody will notice. The fact that by doing this you lose first clarity and then meaning itself is probably beside the point.

That is why *Modern American Usage: A Guide,* by the late Wilson Follett, is such a welcome and important book. I wish that anyone who ever tries to write anything more consequential than a letter to his family might be required to read it, to reread it, and to meditate upon it. Here is a wise, effective, and pleasingly witty attack on sloppy writing and on the things that cause sloppy writing.

Mr. Follett, unfortunately, died before the manuscript was finished. It was edited and completed by Jacques Barzun, with the assistance of some able collaborators, and it is altogether excellent.

Mr. Follett begins with the idea that the noise the violin makes ought not to be dreadful. As he puts it: "... there is a right way to use words and construct sentences, and many wrong ways. The right way is believed to be clearer, simpler, more logical, and hence more likely to prevent error and confusion. Good writing is easier to read; it offers a pleasant combination of sound and sense."

This seems indisputable; but hear Mr. Follett:

Against this majority view is the doctrine of an embattled minority, who make up for their small number by their great learning and their place of authority in the school system and the world of scholarship. They are the professional linguists, who deny that there is such a thing as correctness. The language, they say, is what anybody and everybody speaks. Hence there must be no interference with what they regard as a product of nature; they denounce all attempts at guiding choice; their governing principle is epitomized in the title of a speech by a distinguished member of the profession: "Can Native Speakers of a Language Make Mistakes?"

Well, they can, and do; and Mr. Follett demands "the increasingly obvious and imperative reform—a resumption in our schools of the teaching of grammar and the reading of books." What the writer needs most, he believes, is "the blessing of an orderly mind," because "for all who speak or write, the road to effective language is thinking straight." What you write reflects what you think, and if your writing is fuzzy your thinking is probably fuzzy. But old-style grammar is out of date. We used to believe that any good sentence can be parsed; that is, "it can be broken down into subjects and objects and antecedents, cases and parts of speech, modes and tenses." To do this is a lot of trouble, of course, and I can remember weary hours spent as a grade-school inmate—come to think of it, we used to say "grammar school"—parsing sentences, building intricate sentence-structure diagrams to show subject, predicate, modifying clause, and what not. It was a great bore, and I would have preferred to go fishing,

---

Modern American Usage: A Guide, by Wilson Follett, edited and completed by Jacques Barzun, in collaboration with Carlos Baker, Frederick W. Dupee, Dudley Fitts, James D. Hart, Phyllis McGinley, and Lionel Trilling. Hill & Wang, Inc. 436 pp. $7.50.

---

but it was part of the process of learning the rules: "English does have a structure, a logic at its center, a set of principles, a consistency matching that of the orderly mind. Of this structure grammar is the working diagram and teachable plan—reason enough why, to the worker in prose, grammar remains indispensable."

All of this is very good, but it seems to me that the real riches of this book are found in its lexicon, which constitutes about seven eighths of the text. A few samples may suffice:

Few periods in history have been so reluctant to call things by their right names as our own. Our neighbors do not go crazy, they *become disturbed;* employers no longer fire or discharge employees, they *effect a separation or termination.* Even important warnings come wrapped in cotton wool, not to say couched in falsehoods—witness this printed card put in the bedrooms of a first-class hotel: *For your added comfort and convenience please lock your door and adjust chain before retiring.*

Why, asks Mr. Follett, does it not simply say, "For your safety," and tell you to "fasten" the chain?

The lexicon points out that there are pitfalls from which only a solid knowledge of language and grammar will protect us. There is, for instance, the misuse of *like*—as in the well-known example of the cigarette advertisement. The trouble here is that "the grammatically scared" refuse to use *like* when they ought to use it. As the book points out, "When we ought to write *The Greenland birds, like the mallards, remain in the country in winter,* we must not be done out of *like* by terror lest someone suspect us of meaning *remain . . . in winter like the mallards do.*" Even worse, perhaps, is the misuse—or the timid failure to use—the objective form of the pronoun *who:* "Between those who are afraid of sounding ignorant and those who are afraid of sounding superior, *whom* falls into comparative disuse and causes increasing discomfort in its users." Thus we get such locutions as *I know perfectly well whom you are,* where the writer thinks *whom* is the object of *know* when it is really the subject of *are;* and a sentence reading *Ahead of them on the Nonesuch road they descried Lord Grey de Hilton, whom Essex declared was his enemy.* Mr. Follett's comment here is satisfactory: "One of the paradoxes of the time is that some liberal grammarians who are implacable toward *whom* in its orthodox uses will tie themselves into knots in the effort to condone *whom* in this particular construction. Apparently they have a feeling that it ought to command the blessing of the learned because it tramples on prescriptive grammar."

Then there is the terribly abused word *disinterested.* Maybe the battle here has been lost, but the writers of this book are not ready to give up. Thus:

Disinterest, or *disinterestedness,* as it is now employed by the careless or the desperate, not only blurs the meaning but also stops the reader who can see two possible meanings, because it is still the name of a great, sterling, and positive virtue—freedom from self-seeking motives. It is not the name of a lack, which is what the writer was looking for. *Is one of the consequences of good times a disinterest in bad news?* Here *disinterest* is the wrong word, *uninterestedness* would be a fumbling one. *Indifference* (with *to*) is the inevitable word.

The temptation to go on quoting until closing time is strong, but there are limits. The point I want to make is that this book is an excellent corrective for the sloppiness, imprecision, and frequent unintelligibility of much that passes for writing these days. The English language is one of the most flexible instruments man has devised. Used properly, it can say anything the user wants to say. It cannot be used properly unless one knows something about the governing rules and principles. Although Mr. Follett pours out his scorn on the educationalist's misuse of the word *discipline,* grammar does constitute a *discipline,* in the literal sense, and it is time writers began subjecting themselves to it.

the streets ... and the hatred toward the abolitionists was so bitter and merciless that the friends of Lovejoy [an Illinois antislavery publicist killed by a mob] left his grave long unmarked."

Angelina read of Garrison's ordeal, and she read his own "Appeal"—not for mercy, but for the freedom to go on agitating. She was so moved that she sat down and wrote him a letter. It was a strong statement of support, castigating his critics, including

those high in church and state [who] secretly approve and rejoice over the violent measures [of mobs].... the ground you stand on is holy ground.... If you surrender it, the hope of the slave is extinguished and the chains of his servitude will be strengthened one-hundred-fold. But let no man take your crown, success is as certain as the rising of tomorrow's sun ...

If persecution will abolish slavery, it will also purify the church, and who that stands between the porch and the altar, weeping over the sins of the people, would not be willing to suffer, if such immense good will be accomplished?

She waited several days and prayed for divine guidance before she "felt easy" to send the letter. Once it was committed to the post office, however, she "felt anxiety removed, and as though I had nothing more to do with it."

Garrison printed the whole of it, without comment except to note that the writer was "the daughter of a prominent South Carolina family, a sister of the late Thomas S. Grimké [a well-known reformer in other fields than abolition and leader of the fight against nullification and secession in his state in 1830], and a member of the Philadelphia Society of Friends."

The conservative Friends in Angelina's meeting were outraged. Many believed that her references to "the church" were directed at her own. Even Sarah was shocked at her flouting of the rule which required a Friend to submit any article intended for publication to the elders of his meeting. Angelina was urged to apologize publicly, and to explain that Garrison had printed her letter in the *Liberator* without her permission. She refused.

Sometime during the next few months, Mrs. Grimké wrote to Sarah and Angelina that she was making her will. Angelina, who had exhausted herself and her mother in a futile attempt to convert the latter to abolitionism, wrote back, begging that all Mrs. Grimké's slaves be included in the portions to be bequeathed to her two errant daughters. Surprisingly, Mrs. Grimké obliged. Upon her death, four more were to be added to the growing list of Grimké slaves that Angelina, Sarah, and a third sister—Mrs. Anna Frost

of Philadelphia—had freed and assisted in setting themselves up in the North.

But these and similar small worthy acts were not what Angelina felt she was "being kept for." From girlhood on, she had had intimations that some great work was in store for her. That it was to be connected with the abolition of slavery she was now convinced. But just what it was to be had not yet been made clear.

During the summer of 1836, which she spent with a family of Quakers named Parker in Shrewsbury, New Jersey, she was moved to write "An Appeal to the Christian Women of the South." It was a long, reasoned argument—documented with scriptural references—urging them to act in their own interest and that of their sons, brothers, fathers, and sweethearts while there was yet time.

Elizur Wright, one of the officers of the American Anti-Slavery Society in New York, remembered years afterward that

when the storm of public indignation ... was black upon us, and we were comparatively only a handful, there appeared ... this mild, modest, soft-speaking woman, then in the prime of her beauty, delicate as lily-of-the-valley. She placed in my hands a roll of manuscript, beautifully written. ... It was like a patch of blue sky breaking through that storm cloud.

The society published the "Appeal" as a pamphlet of thirty-six pages, priced at six and a half cents a copy (four dollars for 100), and mailed quantities of them to the South. The reaction of the city of Charleston to this message from its Cassandra launched Angelina on what was to be her great work.

In Charleston and other southern cities, the "Appeal" was officially condemned by the postal authorities and publicly burned, but a mere bonfire did not appease Charlestonians. A rumor spread that Angelina intended to return to spend the winter with her mother. The mayor himself called upon Mrs. Grimké and "desired her to inform her daughter that the police had been instructed to prevent her landing ... that if she should elude their vigilance and go on shore she would be arrested and imprisoned." Friends wrote Angelina, warning her that if she defied the mayor's threat she could not hope to escape personal violence at the hands of a mob.

Here, perhaps, was an opportunity for the martyrdom Angelina had told Garrison she would welcome. She was tempted to try it, "helping thus to reveal to the free states that slavery defies and tramples alike constitutions and laws, and thus outlaws itself." But she could not bring herself to expose her mother and unsympathetic siblings to the same risks, and decided not to go.

While the clamor attendant upon this semiofficial exile was still audible, it occurred to the leaders of the Anti-Slavery Society that if Angelina could bring about such repercussions by writing to the women of the South, she might do even better by speaking to the women of the North. The society sent her an official invitation to come to New York "to hold meetings in private parlors, with Christian women, on the subject of slavery."

Angelina showed the invitation to Sarah, with the comment that she felt it to be "God's call." Sarah was appalled. She begged her sister to consider: that she had never spoken in public, even in meeting, where women were as free as men to speak when the spirit moved them; that she had always had a "morbid shrinking from whatever would make her conspicuous" and she would be going among strangers, wearing the strange garb of the Quakers and speaking in their strange plain speech; that prejudice against women's speaking in public was as widespread as prejudice against abolitionism; and, finally, that if she were to act without the sanction of "the Meeting for Sufferings," her mission might be regarded as "disorderly" and she might be disowned by the Quakers.

Angelina replied that she could not in good conscience ask leave to do something she had already made up her mind to do, that it would be "a grief to me to grieve them [her fellow Friends]," and very unpleasant to be disowned, "but misery to be self-disowned." Sarah's other warnings she brushed aside, asserting that if she was indeed meant to do this thing, strength would be granted her. "The responsibility is thrust upon me," she said. "I cannot thrust it off."

In the end, Sarah capitulated and offered to go with her. Angelina wrote to the Anti-Slavery Society in New York, accepting their invitation but declining the small salary they had offered: she and her sister would travel at their own expense.

 It was at this turning point in her life that Angelina met Theodore Weld. For over a year the Lion of the West, as Garrison called him, had been engaged in a one-man crusade to win the whole territory west of the Hudson and north of the Ohio for abolitionism. But he had overstrained and finally ruined his voice. When the Grimké sisters arrived in New York City in November, 1836, Weld was presiding over an "agents' convention," training a corps of young agitators who were to be sent into the field to take up where he had had to leave off. By special permission, Angelina and Sarah were admitted to these training sessions.

Weld also did some private coaching of the sisters in advance of the first meeting at which they were to speak, a gathering of female abolitionists. In Angelina he discovered a natural talent that needed no training; instead, he helped her with advice about the logical buttressing of the truths she felt so intuitively. For Sarah he could not do much: her delivery was slow, halting, monotonous in tone. But she was a clear thinker, and did not the Book of Ecclesiastes say, "Two are better than one; because they have a good reward for their labor"?

As the day of their first meeting drew closer, opposition to it grew sharper. No public announcement of the sisters' participation had been made, but rumor ran, and interest was so high it was decided to hold the meeting not in a private home but in the vestry of a Baptist church. Angry anonymous letters were dropped in the mailbox of the house where the sisters were lodging. More than one staunch male abolitionist called to advise them to default and spare the already embattled cause the ridicule to which they were exposing it. On the morning of the meeting itself, leaflets were distributed calling on the respectable community to turn out "and teach a lesson to [these] notoriety-seeking females."

The sisters went to Weld for counsel.

"Slavery is on trial," he told them. "The people of the North are the court. You are summoned as witnesses to sustain the prosecution." And although he was fighting certain tender feelings for Angelina which he considered downright wicked in a man in his position—and would have been glad to insulate himself by putting as much distance between them as possible—he escorted her to the very door of the vestry room.

He did not, of course, attend the meeting. The presence of men, even ordained ministers, in any place where women spoke in anything but a conversational tone made an audience "promiscuous" and would have created more scandal. The all-female audience—some 300 crowded into a church vestry that accommodated 100 comfortably—were greeted by the church's minister, who prayed for the success of their enterprise and then beat a quick retreat.

Maria Chapman (a leader in the women's section of the abolition movement from its beginnings) introduced Angelina to the gathering. Angelina rose—and turned deathly pale. What Sarah had foreseen and dreaded was coming to pass: she was paralyzed with stage fright, unable to utter a word. She had not written out her text, and the few notes she had jotted were of no help because her eyes were swimming. All she could gasp out—too faintly to be heard beyond the first row—were some dimly remembered snatches of Scripture: "If I hold my peace, the stone would cry out of the wall, and the beam of the timber would answer it." Then she bowed her head and prayed.

Within moments she was answered by a sudden surge of strength. Words flooded into her mind. It was the first of a series of apparent miracles that occurred at intervals during the fifteen months that followed. The gift of tongues descended upon her. Wendell Phillips later described the scene:

It was not only the testimony of one most competent to speak, but it was the profound religious experience of one who had broken out of the charmed circle.... It was when you saw she was opening some secret record of her own experience that painful silence and breathless interest told the deep effect ... her words were making on minds that afterwards never rested in their work.

When Angelina had finished speaking, Sarah rose and added her testimony, in corroboration. She spoke poorly, but so earnestly that she was not without effectiveness. Before that first meeting was adjourned, a second was announced. It overflowed the vestry room and had to be moved into the church itself. There was a new chorus of outrage, in and out of the pulpit, but the witness of two southern women, once slave-owners themselves, made an impact that could not be shouted down. The sluggish liberal conscience was stirring at last.

 The first Female Anti-Slavery Society in America was formed, and Angelina and Sarah were appointed agents. Calls for the sisters came in from all over the city, and then the state. They spoke at first only to women, but more and more often men appeared at their meetings. At first they were asked politely to leave, but one evening in a Negro church in Poughkeepsie the sisters "felt easy" to speak to "our colored brethren on whose behalf we are laboring."

Next they responded to calls for their services in New England. Men came to the meetings in greater numbers now, and did not always leave when asked. One evening in Lynn, Massachusetts, the sisters spoke to "over a thousand people, packed into the meeting house at some danger to the joists of the flooring." There were more men than women in the crowd. "Yet the heavens did not open to rain thunderbolts on their impious heads!" the local editor remarked, with irony.

What the heavens did not do, some of the New England clergy tried to do for them. Certain clergymen whose congregations had invited the sisters threatened to resign. Sometimes when the sisters arrived at a meeting, they found the church door locked, and had to adjourn to a hall, a home, or a barn. On one occasion, small boys pelted them with apples.

One Reverend Nehemiah Adams grew so incensed

that he composed a pastoral letter that was passed as a resolution by the General Association of Evangelical Clergymen, meeting in Brookfield, Massachusetts. It invited attention to

the dangers which at present seem to threaten the female character with widespread and permanent injury. When a woman assumes the place and tone of man as a public reformer, our care and protection of her seems unnecessary; we put ourselves in self-defense against her; she yields that power which God has given her for protection, and her character becomes unnatural....

The poet John Greenleaf Whittier, who had become a devoted friend of the sisters, was moved to one of his rare satirical verses in rebuttal:

> So this is all! the utmost reach
> Of priestly power the mind to fetter,
> When laymen think, when women preach,
> A war of words, a "Pastoral Letter"!

And now came an attack from an unexpected direction. Catharine Beecher, daughter of the great Lyman, sister of Henry and of Harriet (who had yet to write her best-selling *Uncle Tom's Cabin*), wrote a cutting criticism of the Grimkés' radicalism. Angelina took time off—it must have been stolen from sleep, for she had no idle hours—to answer Miss Beecher in a series of thirteen letters, which Garrison published in the *Liberator*. She was neither gentle nor tactful. "Oh, my very soul is grieved," she wrote at the end of one, "to find a Northern woman thus 'sewing pillows under all armholes,' framing and fitting soft excuses for the slaveholder's conscience, whilst with the same pen she is *professing* to regard slavery as a sin. An open enemy is better than such a secret friend!"

Sarah was also writing letters to the newspapers that winter. Her series on "The Equality of the Sexes and the Condition of Women," which appeared in the Boston *Spectator* and later as a small book, stated her view of the case so forthrightly that fence-straddlers were forced to take sides. But those who were in opposition were not in time to damp the fire the sisters were kindling.

When the Grimkés went through New England, such was the overpowering influence with which they swept the churches that men did not remember the dogma [that women should be silent] till after they had gone. When they left, and the spell weakened, some woke to the idea that it was wrong for a woman to speak to a public assembly. The wakening of old prejudice to its combat with new convictions was a fearful storm.

In February of 1838, before the storm broke, Angelina wound up her New England tour with the most extraordinary exploit of all: she addressed the legislature of the Commonwealth of Massachusetts.

The occasion was the presentation of some petitions to Congress asking that slavery be abolished in the District of Columbia. Ex-President John Quincy Adams, now a member of the House of Representatives, was waging a battle for the right to petition, and the New England abolitionists had labored long and hard to amass an impressive number of signatures (see "Mad Old Man from Massachusetts" in the April, 1961, AMERICAN HERITAGE). It occurred to Henry Stanton (who was later to marry the redoubtable feminist Elizabeth Cady) that since many of the signatures had been obtained at meetings where Angelina spoke, she might be one of the speakers at the official presentation ceremony before the state legislature. He made the suggestion half in jest, for of course no woman had ever been heard there, and it was not likely that permission for such an innovation would be granted. But Angelina accepted the challenge.

She applied to the legislators for permission to address them not as a representative of the Anti-Slavery Society "but as a woman, as a Southerner, as a moral being." The permission was granted, and she was scheduled to speak after the last of the male abolitionists.

When she and Sarah arrived at the statehouse that day, they could hardly get up the stairs, and the legislative chamber itself was so packed that they had to walk over the tops of desks to reach their seats. All the women abolitionists had come, depending on Angelina to "do something important for women, for our country, and for the whole world." The moment was upon her, but the spirit was not stirring. She suddenly went so pale that Sarah thought she would faint.

Angelina bowed her head and prayed, but nothing happened. Her mind was still empty, except of wonder at the arrogance that had prompted her to volunteer. She was called upon by the chairman of the Committee on Petitions, and she managed to get to her feet and begin.

Her voice was so weak that the chairman could not hear her, and he interrupted to invite her to come forward and stand at his secretary's desk, which occupied a raised platform just below his own desk and which faced the chamber. Angelina obeyed.

At this point a great hissing broke out at one of the doors in the rear of the room. Opposition always had a calming effect on Angelina, and she began again, with more firmness than before. But since her back was still to the chairman, and he still could not hear her, he interrupted once more to invite her to come up to his place, which was that of the speaker of the house. By the time she and Sarah (who would not leave her) were "ensconced in the seats of the mighty," Angelina had entirely recovered her self-confidence.

Her address lasted two hours. Her voice was as strong as a man's, but toward the end the quiet was so complete that she could have been heard if she had only whispered. At adjournment time she had not covered all her points, so she asked for permission to be heard again. Permission was granted and a day set for her second appearance. Again she spoke to a packed house, this time without hecklers. Again she did not finish, and a third hearing was arranged.

By this time public interest was so intense that the galleries of the statehouse could not begin to hold all who wanted to hear her. The Odeon Theatre was rented, and a series of six lectures by Angelina was announced.

Nothing like this had ever happened in the history of abolitionism, and news of it spread to other cities —among them Philadelphia, where Angelina was going to be married as soon as she caught her breath and quieted her overwrought nerves.

This marriage and the love affair that led up to it was the best-kept secret of its day. Theodore Weld had been "half in love" with Miss Angelina from the day he read her letter to Garrison in the *Liberator*, and his first glimpse of her in the flesh completed the conquest. But he had taken a vow—only half in earnest, but in public—never to marry "until the last slave was free." Also, he was penniless, in broken health, and without a profession that gave him hope of being able to support a wife—least of all a wife who had been raised in the lap of southern luxury. He did his stern best to root what he regarded as this "guilty passion" out of his heart, and his apparent coldness forced Angelina to keep her own feelings concealed.

But they had kept up a correspondence all during her New England campaign. Weld wrote to both sisters, advising them on tactics and arguments, and subjecting their behavior, their characters, and their writings to the most critical scrutiny—a practice among devout persons which went by the euphemism "being faithful." Gradually Weld's attacks on Angelina began to reflect the depth of his feeling—in reverse. At last he went too far and she rebelled.

And yet, Brother, I think in some things you wronged me in that letter never to be forgotten, but never mind, YOU DID NOT HURT ME, even that did me good.... Be sure to keep that letter of mine which you said I ought to be ashamed of—all the rest better be destroyed. There will be no use in writing about it—WE CAN NOT UNDERSTAND EACH OTHER, and I have unintentionally said too much perhaps...

When Theodore realized that he had wounded her, he lost control of himself. There was no way to explain his rudeness except by confessing his love. Angelina responded by declaring hers, and it was only by keeping apart for the time being that either was able to get on with the all-important work.

They planned to be married as soon as Angelina had finished her lectures at the Odeon, i.e., in a matter of a few weeks. No one but Sarah was taken into their confidence. Angelina was, for the moment, the most talked-about woman in America, and the news that she was engaged to be married would have transformed the Odeon series into a side show, or so she feared. (Even her partisans considered that Angelina's public life had by now unfitted her forever for the role of a good wife and mother.) The lovers were so discreet that not even Whittier, who shared an office with Theodore, and Henry Stanton, who lived with him, knew what was afoot until they received their invitations to what was undoubtedly the most extraordinary wedding they would ever attend.

They and other friends and members of Theodore's family (Angelina's were invited but did not respond) gathered on the evening of May 14, 1838, in the parlor at the home of Angelina's sister, Anna Grimké Frost, who lived in Philadelphia, to hear the bride and groom speak the vows *they* had decided upon, and to ask—without the assistance of a minister—the blessing of God on their union. The date had been chosen to coincide with the dedication ceremonies of Pennsylvania Hall, which many out-of-town abolitionists were expected to attend. Philadelphia had been chosen for the additional reason that by Pennsylvania law a marriage was legal if the couple did no more than announce, in the presence of twelve witnesses, their intention to live together in the future as man and wife. It was not "registered" unless one of the latter was also a notary, and Weld had taken pains not to invite one: had the marriage been registered, he would have had a legal claim to all Angelina's worldly goods, including her inheritance to come, and that would have made him uncomfortable.

The evening was what Sarah called "a true love feast." Angelina and Theodore glowed like lamps and spread warmth in all directions. The guest list included black and white, rich and poor, freeborn and ex-slave, and the leaders of diverse factions in the abolition movement, meeting under truce for perhaps the last time. Garrison performed the one official act required by the state: the reading aloud of the marriage certificate. Whittier had to wait outside till that was over, lest he be disowned—as Angelina and Sarah were soon to be—for attending a non-Quaker wedding. But he was called in for the cutting of the cake, which had been baked by one of the guests, an ex-slave of Anna Grimké Frost's. (It contained only non-slave-produced sugar, which was not easy to come by.)

Two nights later, on May 16, the bride was sched-uled to speak at Pennsylvania Hall. The program was designed to take advantage of public curiosity about lady abolitionists, principally Angelina herself. All the speakers, therefore, were to be women—except for Garrison, who had asked for a chance to apologize for the personal attack he had made on a local "gradualist" in his speech at the dedication.

Something in the temper of the neighborhood—which was near the waterfront—made the sponsors uneasy, and they called on the mayor well in advance to request protection on behalf of the "many ladies who would be present." The mayor was shocked at such a lack of confidence in "the good sense and good manners of their fellow Philadelphians." And indeed, as the audience began to gather, the apprehensions of the abolitionists were lulled by the appearance of so many well-dressed and apparently well-behaved gentlemen.

They had expected more women to be among them, and more of the local faithful, but by the time these arrived, all the seats had been taken. It was regrettable that so many had to be turned away, but it was good to carry the message to ears that had not already heard it. As the meeting began, a crowd was gathering in the street . . . .

Garrison spoke first and was hissed, which angered him so that he forgot his apology and spoke more intemperately than before. When he had finished, Maria Chapman came to the podium. As if at a signal, boos and catcalls were heard from every part of the hall, and stones thrown from the street below began to shatter the windows along one side of the room.

Too late, the abolitionists realized that they had fallen into a trap. No police were anywhere to be seen. The hall was packed with blood brothers of the mob outside. Provocators were stationed at all strategic points, and the crowd was so dense that it was impossible to eject anyone. It was also impossible for any speaker to be heard. Quite possibly something—anything—might start a panic that would send people stampeding toward the exit doors, trampling and crushing the just along with the unjust.

At this moment Angelina came forward and held up

her hand for silence. The hubbub inside quieted, and she managed to make herself heard over the noise from outside.

"Men! Brothers and fathers! Mothers and daughters and sisters! What came ye out for to see? A reed shaken in the wind?"

Stones continued to strike and break the windows. Glass continued to fall in the aisle and on the stage. The mob outside continued to scream threats. But inside the hall Angelina had established her supremacy.

"What is a mob?" she asked. "What would the breaking of every window be? Any evidence that we are wrong or that slavery is a good and wholesome institution?

"There is nothing to fear from those who would stop our mouths. . . . If the arm of the North had not already caused the bastille of slavery to totter, you would not hear those cries."

From this extemporized beginning, Angelina worked her way back to the address she had planned to give. It took her over an hour to finish. When she could not make herself heard over the noise from the street, she waited for it to subside, and then went on. When stones landed on the stage or among her listeners, she made reference to them if it suited her point, or ignored them if it did not. And, at last, she called upon the audience, beginning with the women on the platform, to form in ranks of two and follow her out of the building and through the mob in the street.

It was an inspired tactic. Any attempt on the part of the abolitionist men to protect the women would probably have triggered an assault—inside or outside the hall. But the thin line of women, led by the slender, gray-gowned bride, seemed to shame the rowdies. They stepped aside and made an aisle through which Angelina walked. After her came the women, and after them the men. Even the proslavery men who had come to heckle Angelina marched out in silent sobriety. The mob was quiet until the last of them had passed. Not until the next evening did the planned outrage take place. The police were still absent when the mob returned to sack and burn Pennsylvania Hall, the sanctuary that had just been dedicated to freedom.

That was the last time Angelina Grimké Weld was heard in a public place. She retired with her husband to a small New Jersey farm to learn, under the most trying of conditions, the domestic lessons she had missed. She and Sarah (who lived with the Welds for the rest of her life) took up the burdens of housekeeping while Theodore wrestled with the farm from spring to fall, and spent his winters in Washington as consultant and lobbyist for the abolition faction in Congress. Angelina in her middle and late thirties bore three children in five years and suffered long, painful illnesses after each of the births. She never recovered her health.

There were calls for her services during those first years, but she was never able to respond, and after a while the calls became infrequent. She did try, once or twice, to address very small, informal groups of women, but the effort was enormous and the result disappointing. The gift of tongues had been taken from her. The one task of any importance that she did undertake was helping her husband with his great documentary pamphlet, *American Slavery As It Is*, for which she and Sarah read and clipped southern newspapers and wrote moving testimonies of their own.

As the years rolled on, the Welds and Sarah became more and more occupied with the tasks of earning a living and raising the children. The movement to which they had given their best years split and split again. The Welds managed to keep friendships on both sides, mainly because of their isolation. For a while they ran a boarding school at Eagleswood, a utopian community in New Jersey, to which many abolitionists and transcendentalists sent their children. Teaching became their principal occupation, and at the end of the Civil War Angelina and Theodore found places in Dr. Lewis' school at Fairmount, Massachusetts, one of the first schools to admit Negro students.

 In the enforced quiet of this life, Angelina had found a sort of peace. Now the chance reading of an article in a newspaper threatened to shatter that peace and make demands on a strength that she no longer possessed—at least in a physical sense. Archibald Grimké's answer to her was dated February 20, 1868:

Dear Madam:

I was somewhat surprised by receiving yours of the 15th inst. I never expected to hear through the medium of a letter from "Miss Angelina Grimké" of anti-Slavery celebrity . . .

I shall proceed to give you a simple sketch of my history and my connections:

I am the son of Henry Grimké, a brother of Dr. John Grimké, & therefore your brother. . . . He was married to a Miss Simons . . . & she died, leaving three children . . . After her death he took my mother, who was his slave & his children's nurse; her name was Nancy Weston. . . . By my mother he had three children, viz Archibald, which is my name, Francis & John. . . . He told my mother that he could not free her . . . "but," said he, "I leave you better than free, because I leave you to be taken care of."

Mr. E. M. Grimké [Henry's son] did not do as his father commanded, and [my mother] was thrown upon the uncharitable world to struggle ... alone. By dint of hard labor she kept us from perishing by hunger ... until 1860, when Mr. E. M. Grimké married a second time ... & he wanted a boy to wait on him. He informed my mother that she should send me to his house.... Thus he kept on until she was rendered childless.... I afterwards fled from my oppressor. Frank attempted to escape but was retaken & sold. ...

[When] Freedom was proclaimed to all men ... the disjointed members of our little family were united ... the public schools were flung open to all. I ... went to one of them and through the intercessions [of Mrs. Pillsbury, the principal] we [he and Frank] were admitted here ... My younger bro. is at home with my mother. He cannot get a support, hence he cannot come ...

 Angelina was devastated, not by the news that she had Negro nephews, but by the guilt of her brother, who had sired children and left them in bondage, and of her white nephew, who had taken advantage of the bequest to enslave and ultimately to sell his own half-brother. She suffered one of her "prostrations"—blinding headaches, double or blurred vision, periods of faintness and dizziness—so severe and protracted that she had to give up her teaching and take to her bed. But by February 29 she had composed her answer to the nephews:

Dear young friends:

I cannot express the mingled emotions with which I perused your deeply interesting and touching letter. The facts it disclosed were *no* surprise to me. Indeed, had I not suspected that you might be my nephews, I should probably not have addressed you ...

I will not dwell on the past: let all that go. It cannot be altered. Our work is in the present and duty calls upon us now so to use the past as to convert its curse into a blessing. I am glad you have taken the name of Grimké. It was *once* one of the noblest names of Carolina. ... It was the grief of my heart that during the late war, not one of the name of Grimké—neither man nor woman—was found on the side of loyalty & freedom, all bow'd down together & worshipped Slavery—"the Mother of all Abominations."

You, my young friends, now bear this once honored name. I charge you most solemnly, by your upright conduct and your life-long devotion to the eternal principles of justice and humanity and religion, to lift this name out of the dust where it now lies, and set it once more among the princes of our land.

Angelina did not let the matter rest there. As soon as she was able she set out for Oxford, Pennsylvania, to meet her nephews face to face, and to acknowledge them publicly as "the sons of my brother, Henry Grimké, and his wife, Nancy Weston Grimké." She inquired into their plans and ambitions and learned that they wanted to prepare themselves for professional careers. She offered all the financial assistance

she and Sarah were capable of (which was not much at the time), and invited the boys to visit her in Fairmount. Archibald's daughter, in a memoir of her father, later described the visit:

They went ... To the boys this was a great occasion, the greatest in all their lives, and cost what it might, they were determined to live up to it. They were virtually penniless, but each carried a cane, wore a high silk hat which had been made to order and boots that were custom-made. Whatever the aunts and the Welds thought, they were welcomed with wide open arms and hearts and made at home. The simplicity here soon taught them their lesson.

The boys graduated from Lincoln in 1870 with the highest honors, Frank as class valedictorian. Both returned for the master's degree. Archibald then went on to Harvard Law School and Frank to the law department of Howard University in Washington. The Welds not only helped Archibald with tuition money but also with contacts that eventually led to his establishment in a Boston law firm. Sarah made a special effort on Frank's behalf: in her late seventies she undertook a verse translation of a French work on Joan of Arc to earn a part of his tuition money.

Sarah died at the age of eighty-one in 1873, the year Frank entered Howard; Angelina lived another six years and saw Frank change his field from the law to the ministry, enter and graduate from Princeton Theological Seminary, and go to his first church, the Fifteenth Street Presbyterian in Washington. She did not live to appreciate the tribute of Archibald's naming his first and only child Angelina Weld Grimké in loving memory of her.

In the ministry, Frank found a vocation that fulfilled him completely. He married Charlotte Forten, a remarkable woman who had served as the only Negro teacher in the first freedmen's schools established by the Union Army on the Carolina coast. The couple had only one child, a daughter, who died young. Frank was associated with his brother in the cause of Negro advancement, but the thrust of his life was in his ministry. Four volumes of his sermons have been collected and published by Carter Woodson, whose editorial comment on the Reverend Mr. Grimké's career would have delighted both the aunts: "All who knew him were not his followers. He alienated the genuflecting, compromising, and hypocritical leaders of both races ... A man of high ideals, who lived above reproach and bore an honorable name even among those who did not agree with him.... Persons who knew him well often referred to him as the Black Puritan ..."

Archibald did not find a single vocation, financial security, or much sustained personal happiness. He was intelligent, diligent, and extremely personable, but it took more than that to make a living in the law in Boston in the 1880's and 90's—if one was also a Negro. Archibald undertook a number of other tasks; some paid, others did not. He edited a Negro weekly called *The Hub,* and wrote occasional articles for the large Boston dailies. The high point of his career was his tour of duty as United States Consul to Santo Domingo (1894–98).

He served from 1903 to 1916 as president of the American Negro Academy and joined William E. B. Dubois in the Niagara Movement and in the National Association for the Advancement of Colored People, which grew out of it.

His marriage (to a white woman) was a failure and left deep emotional scars on him and on his daughter, who was at first taken from him by her mother, then—at the age of seven—returned to him to raise. His financial situation was always so strained as to amount to genteel poverty, and until in his last years he became a member of his brother's household, he never really had a home. But his long effort was recognized —in 1919, in his seventieth year—by the award of the N.A.A.C.P.'s highest honor, the Spingarn Medal, for distinguished achievement and service to his race.

Angelina's charge was not laid on her two Negro nephews to no effect. They did indeed do honor to the Grimké name.

Sisters and Brothers, Janet Stevenson's novel on the Grimkés and their Negro nephews, was published recently by Crown. She has written two other historical novels, Weep No More *and* The Ardent Years, *as well as studies of John James Audubon and Marian Anderson. Miss Stevenson is presently teaching English at Grambling College in Louisiana.*

The Passion of Hernando de Soto CONTINUED FROM PAGE 31

twelve exhausted Indians were still treading water defiantly. De Soto ordered his best swimmers to fish them out and had them put in chains. De Soto had proved his point—his troops were infinitely superior in open battle. Unfortunately for the Spanish, this was the only occasion on which de Soto was able to show his flair and courage as a field commander.

The army spent the winter in an open area near modern Tallahassee. The local inhabitants had fled, leaving behind their well-filled grain bins and fields of standing crops. The Spanish soldiers harvested beans, pumpkins, walnuts, and plums, and built a fortified camp. A cavalry patrol reported that the Gulf coast was only eight leagues away. On the beach they had found the last traces of Narváez's expedition —crosses carved on trees, mangers hollowed from tree trunks, and the skulls of horses. De Soto ordered up the men from the base camp at Tampa, and his supply fleet arrived with fresh provisions. When these had been landed, the general sent his ships back to Cuba, except for one caravel, which he dispatched westward along the coast to find a good harbor. The caravel returned in February, having located an excellent harbor in Pensacola Bay; and it was arranged that her captain would return there with the supply fleet the following autumn to greet the expeditionary force after its second summer in the field.

The Spaniards had spent a miserable winter under daily harassment from the natives, but now they were cheered by news of a queen, in a land far to the east, who received tribute of furs and gold from all the surrounding tribes. A native prisoner who claimed to be one of her subjects even demonstrated how the yellow metal was dug from the ground, melted, and refined. The Spanish soldiers could hardly wait to invade this promised land, and on March 3, 1540, the army of Florida began marching into the pinelands of what is now Georgia.

It was a terrible journey. They were hacking their way through trackless forests which even the Indians shunned. Food ran out, porters starved to death or were sent back to lessen the number of mouths to feed, men-at-arms threw away much of their armor, horses died. The usual food ration was a handful of parched grain each day. De Soto ordered some of the hogs to be killed, but the issue of half a pound of meat per man scarcely eased the situation.

Near the northern border of Georgia, the army found its tribute-collecting queen, the princess of Cofitachequi. But she was a sad disappointment. Her gold turned out to be burnished copper, and her slabs of silver were sheets of mica. The only booty was a heap of river pearls extracted from fresh-water mussels, but most of these were ruined by boring or discolored by fire. The Spaniards collected 350 pounds of the pearls and left in disgust. According to legend, one of the "dark men" stayed behind to marry the princess and rule as lord of Cofitachequi.

Through the southern part of present-day South Carolina, into North Carolina, Tennessee, and northern Alabama, de Soto led his army, as the summer of 1540 wore on. One mountain ridge after another had to be climbed; each river looked the same as the previous one they had forded. The maps that the six-

When de Soto sailed from Spain in April, 1538, many thousands of his countrymen came to cheer him on his way.

teenth-century geographers afterward pieced together from the expedition's diaries show a random scattering of Indian villages, mountains, and rivers that reveals the lack of topographic variety.

And still the fortune hunters found no fortunes. As the hopes of the Spaniards declined, their discipline began to sag, particularly among the foot soldiers, who bore the brunt of the hardships. One by one they began to desert, slipping away at night to seek an oblivious life of ease among the natives. De Soto was obliged to post sentries at night to guard against desertions. He could not allow his army to stop for rest. At each village a show of force persuaded the Indian chief to co-operate in providing food, shelter, and porters. If the soldiers wanted women, a few mirrors, combs, and other trinkets were considered a fair trade. Before the expedition left a settlement, de Soto would arrest the chief and take him along as a hostage to prevent an attack on the rear of his line of march. It was a callous policy which, sooner or later, would anger a warlike tribe.

The Indians who struck back at the Spanish were the Choctaw of south-central Alabama. De Soto entered their territory early in October, and was greeted by their chief, Tuscaloosa, the Black Warrior. It was an impressive meeting: the Spanish general clad in armor on his charger and the Indian chief seated on a pile of cushions, wearing a full-length mantle of feathers. Tuscaloosa greeted de Soto warily, but seemed willing to let the Spaniards cross his lands. De Soto responded in his usual high-handed style. He accepted the offer and then ordered his halberdiers to seize Tuscaloosa and take him with the column. It was a fatal mistake; Tuscaloosa managed to send runners to his war chiefs, summoning them to his capital at Mobila,* where they

*This Indian town, probably located near the juncture of the Alabama and Tombigbee rivers in present-day Alabama, has been variously spelled Mavila, Mauvila, Mabila, etc.

set an ambush for de Soto and his soldiers.

When Tuscaloosa told him that Mobila held ample supplies of food, de Soto decided to march on the capital. He moved straight into the trap; to make matters worse, he allowed his troops to disperse and forage. When the main column reached the town, de Soto was accompanied by fifteen troopers and a huge, surly mob of slaves, hostages, and prisoners. Despite the warnings of a Spanish spy who told de Soto that Mobila was swarming with Choctaw warriors, the stiff-necked general decided to enter the town with Tuscaloosa at his side. As the handful of Spaniards passed through the gates, their attention was diverted by a team of dancing girls stationed there as decoys. Then Tuscaloosa signalled his braves to attack, and they rushed out from the houses. De Soto and his companions backed toward the gate with blows ringing off their armor. Five of the white men were hacked to pieces protecting their general, and de Soto himself narrowly escaped.

De Soto's life was saved, but his negligence was still to prove the ruin of his expedition. The Indians in the baggage train had seized their opportunity to escape. They had streamed into Mobila, taking with them all the Spanish supplies, spare weapons, and gunpowder. By the time the main body of the Spanish army arrived, the situation was desperate. On the other side of Mobila's palisades lay all the equipment needed to survive the march down to the coast. Already the ramparts were lined with self-liberated slaves, jeering and holding up their booty to mock the white men.

For de Soto there was no alternative: he had to capture Mobila and regain his equipment. The siege lasted all day, and it was a blood bath. The Spanish infantry hurled themselves against the palisades, hacking at the logs with axes, but were beaten back by the crazed Choctaw. Finally de Soto had to fire the town and risk his equipment in the conflagration. Mobila was built of wood and straw, and it burned like tinder. But with the flames behind them and the halberdiers in front, the Choctaw warriors refused to surrender. They stubbornly resisted and inflicted heavy casualties. De Soto himself received an arrow in the rump and spent the rest of the battle standing in his stirrups. The siege became a massacre of the Choctaw, but not until their last warrior had hanged himself from the ramparts with his own bowstring did the fighting stop, and by then it was clear that the Spanish equipment had burned with the town.

The battle was a victory for the Spanish, but a victory they could not afford. In addition to losing their matériel, they had 22 dead and 148 wounded, some with multiple arrow wounds. Scarcely any soldiers had come through unscathed; they were burned, hungry, and exhausted. De Soto had put himself in an impossible tactical position and had paid the price for his stupidity. By rights, his Florida expedition was finished; they should all have limped to the coast to rendezvous with the ships. But that was not de Soto's style. He was stubbornly convinced that somewhere in Tierra Florida he would build his empire, and he was too proud to return to Spain a failure. When a messenger arrived to report that the supply fleet was waiting, he suppressed the news, fearing that the men would desert and make for the coast. By sheer force of character, de Soto led his men away from their salvation and took them, ill equipped and battered, into the interior for three more years of fighting. The fleet waited in vain to provide them with fresh supplies. Then it sailed back to Cuba, not knowing what had become of the Florida expedition.

The siege of Mobila changed de Soto and changed his army. After the disaster the general became morose and spent more time alone, brooding over his plans. With the loss of the baggage, the army took on the appearance of a gang of buccaneers. At first the natives stayed clear of this wild-eyed rabble of men; they had been shaken by the ferocity at Mobila and did not wish to tackle the Spanish again. But as de Soto moved across the country, his route took him into the territory of the Chickasaw Indians, who had never yet seen a white man and were famous for their valor. The Chickasaw resented de Soto's constant demands for food, blankets, and furs. They planned an attack and waited their opportunity. De Soto, however, was a chastened leader; he was more cautious and more watchful. It was Luis de Moscoso, master of the camp and thus the one responsible for posting the sentries, who gave the Chickasaw their chance.

Moscoso was one of de Soto's favorites. He had been with him in Peru, and even though one of de Soto's homeward-bound treasure ships had been wrecked through Moscoso's negligence, de Soto had forgiven him and had made him chief lieutenant of the Florida expedition. On the night of March 3, 1541, he failed to set a trustworthy guard around the Spanish bivouac.

Several hundred armed Chickasaw warriors succeeded in creeping within range of the camp, each carrying a firebrand concealed in an earthenware pot. It is said that each Indian also carried three ropes—one for a Christian, one for a horse, and one for a pig. The fire attack was a complete surprise. The camp was in flames while the dazed soldiers still fumbled with breastplates and helmets. The sparks set alight the pigsty, and almost three hundred squealing pigs roasted to death. Only the piglets managed to wriggle through the bars; the air smelled of roast pork, while, according to one account, the bacon grease flowed out over the ground. De Soto buckled on his armor and rallied his men. The horses broke loose, and the thunder of their stampede terrified the Chickasaw, who fled, leaving the Spanish battling the flames.

When the fire was extinguished, de Soto saw the smouldering debris of his expedition. It was a worse disaster than Mobila. A dozen Spaniards had been killed or had burned to death, and fifty or sixty horses had been lost. The last surviving white woman was dead. Almost every shred of their blankets and garments had been burned; the men were almost naked, and there was nothing to protect them from the cold nights. Nearly all the metal weapons had been ruined, having lost their temper in the inferno, and all the saddlery was wrecked. Everything wooden was now a charred mass—saddles, lance shafts, axe and pike handles. The Chickasaw had not lost a single warrior.

Under these appalling conditions, the Spaniards were at their best. Their resilience was extraordinary. Working furiously for the next two weeks, they rigged up a crude forge and, using rough bellows made from bear skins and musket barrels, retempered sword blades, crossbows, pike heads, and armor. They salvaged every scrap of metal from the cinders and cut lance shafts from the nearest grove of trees. The runaway horses were rounded up and equipped with rope harnesses made from twisted grass. The men scavenged for skins and grass mats to make sleeping bags and kilts. By the time the Chickasaw returned to the attack, the Spaniards were in fighting trim and easily defeated their enemy.

Moscoso was demoted for his negligence, but there was little time for recriminations. De Soto realized that it was essential to leave Chickasaw territory before his command was wiped out by this warrior tribe. Accordingly the army of Florida gathered together the homemade gear and moved westward as fast as their wounds and burns would allow.

In early May, de Soto's westward path brought him through forest and swamplands to the bank of a huge river, bigger by far than any river they had ever seen in Europe or Mexico. The date was Sunday, May 8, 1541, and the army had been in the field for two years. The river was the Mississippi.

The arrival of the exploring Europeans on the banks of the Mississippi was indeed a historic moment, but the actual scene was vastly different from the romantic version shown in the famous William Henry Powell painting that hangs in the rotunda of the Capitol in Washington (see page 27). The river, in fact, was hidden by a thick, dank forest, probably of cypress and oak. Straggling in untidy groups through the willow thickets, the Spaniards found themselves looking across a huge expanse of water flowing from right to left across their line of march. Later the Father of Waters was to be the lifeline that saved the bulk of the army, but at first glimpse its only real distinction was its immense size. The army's chroniclers immediately called the river the "Rio Grande." The sheer width of so large a body of flowing water has always staggered the European observer; and it must have been all the more huge to de Soto's men, most of whom came from the arid Iberian Peninsula, where such monstrous rivers are geographical impossibilities.

Gazing across at the far bank, a low line of green forest two miles away, de Soto and his men felt sure that this must be the giant river they had heard rumors of in Spain and Cuba, rumors added to by tales from their guides. They hoped it might lead them to some tribe of valley Indians rich in precious metals and gems; but for the time being the Mississippi was, first and foremost, a tiresome obstacle to their march. Ferry boats had to be built, and that would delay the army.

The army was truly a remarkable sight, but not for its pomp and splendor: de Soto, lean and unkempt, sitting loose in the short stirrups of his high wooden saddle, his horse scrawny and jaded; the gaunt soldiers hollow-cheeked and unshaven. Most of the men were dressed in ponchos and kilts of dried grass, though a few luckier ones could boast padded cotton surcoats or rough breeches made from animal skins bald with wear. The priests had lost all their clerical garments and now were dressed like the other men; only a crude cross daubed on their buckskins with ocher set them apart. There were hungry, exhausted Indian porters stooped under ungainly wicker panniers filled with corn and nuts; here and there were war dogs, fierce and lean after months of ill treatment and semistarvation, and scarred from battles. There was not a single piece of shining armor to be seen anywhere: cuirasses, helms, morions, arquebuses, and swords were dented or rusted; homemade lance shafts were crooked; saddle frames were crude and ugly. Yet this was a unique army. Hounded by bad luck, it had lived and fought for thirty-five months across thousands of miles of hostile territory. It had survived two major disasters that by rights should have sent it packing for civilization. This lone Spanish expedition had ranged more widely than the fiercest war party had dreamed of, farther even than the Spanish authorities in Madrid had imagined possible—all this without reinforcements or extra supplies from its base in Cuba. By the time the Florida expedition reached the bank of the Mississippi it was a hardened, self-reliant band.

Near present-day Sunflower Landing in the state of Mississippi the Spaniards spent the next month building ferry barges. For once, food was a minor problem, for the "Rio Grande" swarmed with fish, but there was real danger from the Indians. Not long after the Spanish arrived, Indians came from the far bank in an armada of about two hundred war canoes, each moving in time to the commands of a captain in the stern. Archers stood in the bow of each canoe, and the whole fleet was controlled by a chief who sat on cushions under an awning in the lead vessel. De Soto ordered his crossbowmen to warn them off. The Indians received the salvo with dignified composure and put about in an orderly maneuver: no paddlers broke rhythm but those struck down by crossbow bolts. Every afternoon thereafter the Indian armada put in an appearance at long range and fired arrows at the boatbuilders. No one was hurt, but the construction of the barges was delayed and everyone in the army worried about the crossing.

De Soto knew that if the disciplined Indian war fleet caught his boats in midstream, the Spanish would be annihilated. The men-at-arms rowing the unwieldy barges would be hampered by their cargo of horsemen; all would be at the mercy of the faster Indian dugouts. When the barges were finished, therefore, de Soto had them towed about a mile upstream under cover of night. Catching the Indians completely off guard, he managed to get an advance party across the river without opposition. Once a beachhead was established, the ferries shuttled back and forth with the remainder of the men. By noon the entire army of Florida was safely on the far side of the Mississippi and ready to advance.

As soon as his forces had regrouped, de Soto decided to move strongly against the Indians, whose highly organized war fleet indicated that they might be a rich and sophisticated tribe. This was to be done by land; but first the barges had to be dismantled and every precious iron spike and nail salvaged. When they started upstream, the Spaniards found the terrain along the river the worst imaginable. After a few days of pushing through a water-logged maze of swamps, ponds, oxbow lakes, and mudflats, de Soto led his force away from the river to firmer ground on the inland bluffs. The drier uplands were thickly settled by Casqui Indians, who were enemies of the riparian tribes and welcomed the Spanish as allies against their traditional foes. Too weak to rebuff the Casqui offer of friendship, de Soto for once treated the natives civilly, and they clamored to be baptized so that they too would enjoy the magical properties of the cross, which they believed would deflect the arrows of any enemy. At the same time, they regarded the white-skinned commander as a child of their sun god and insisted on bringing forth their maimed and crippled for de Soto to heal. They even suggested that the Spanish leader invoke his Father to put an end to the drought that was parching their crops. Luckily for de Soto, a heavy thundershower soon afterward enhanced his reputation.

On June 26, 1541, the Spanish and Casqui combined forces for an attack on the neighboring Quapaw tribe, which had its capital at a strongly fortified village on a backwater of the Mississippi. But when it became clear to de Soto that the Quapaw chief was no more than a local ruler and had no gold in his village, he decided not to risk lives needlessly and concluded a peace treaty without delay, sealing it by accepting two Quapaw princesses as concubines. One of the girls, according to an eyewitness, was "well proportioned, tall of body and well fleshed, in her shape and face she looked a lady of high rank," but her sister was merely "strongly made."

The story of the army's wanderings west of the Mississippi from July, 1541, to March, 1542, repeats the history of the previous two years. The Spaniards sent cavalry patrols in all directions, hoping to find the elusive treasure troves; they refused to admit that Florida was barren. It was a brave but useless effort. The Spanish saw bison and met tepee-dwelling nomads who were always poor and usually hostile. They marched countless miles over broken terrain, fought their way out of ambushes, and struggled to survive in the harsh countryside. Physical strain, poor food, disease, and warfare gradually whittled away the army. Once again soldiers began to desert, including some

of the nobly born officers, but this time de Soto was too tired and dispirited to do anything about it.

They spent the winter of 1541–42 at a village near the junction of two rivers, probably the Canadian and the Arkansas, in what is now Oklahoma. Somehow the men made themselves comfortable enough, using buffalo robes for blankets and snaring rabbits for food. De Soto, taking no chances, built an impregnable stockade and cleared away the surrounding underbrush so that the natives could not launch any more sneak attacks. It was here that Juan Ortiz, the Florida castaway, finally died, leaving de Soto without a reliable interpreter of any kind.

Ortiz's death brought home to de Soto his terrible isolation. For month after month the general had been leading his men on a wild-goose chase, searching for mythical cities of gold. His army had proved that it could still travel, but it was desperately short of equipment. There was not a trained geographer, map maker, or navigator in the entire group. If they continued west they might reach Spanish Mexico; on the other hand, they might perish in the Texas deserts which the Indians had told them about. There was still a chance that if they marched to the Gulf coast they could build boats or follow the shore line until they came to a Spanish settlement.

After weeks of brooding and black depression, de Soto made up his mind. They would strike for the Gulf coast and try to get a small barge through to Cuba to bring back the supply fleet. The expedition broke camp and set out to the southeast heading back toward the Mississippi, which they hoped to reach near its mouth. But de Soto had lost his bearings.

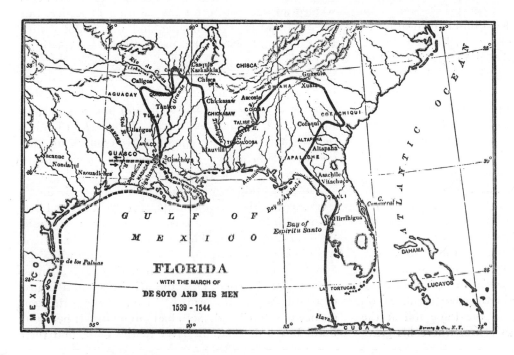

To this nineteenth-century map roughly tracing the route of the army under de Soto, an X has been added to mark the approximate spot of his death on the Mississippi, as well as a dotted line to indicate the route to Mexico taken by his lieutenant, Luis de Moscoso: an aborted overland attempt, and then a successful retreat by water.

When they came within sight of the river and learned that the local Indians had never heard of the Gulf, they were cruelly disappointed. Though they did not know it, they were three hundred miles in a straight line from the Gulf and even farther by the winding river route.

One suspects that at this moment de Soto's stubborn nature finally collapsed. He had invested his fortune and his own life in the Florida expedition. For three years he had not spared himself; he had carried the entire burden of command and shared the hardships of the most humble men-at-arms. Now his force was reduced to about three hundred effective men and only forty horses, many of which were lame after going unshod for a whole year because of the shortage of metal. De Soto lashed out in anger: When the Indians of the area, Guachoya of the river, sensed the Spanish despair, they sent messengers to taunt the invaders; whereupon de Soto ordered his troops to teach the Indians a lesson. His officers, harassed and nervous, exceeded their instructions, and a massacre ensued. It was the worst blot on de Soto's record, one which in later years his enemies in Spain would use to discredit his memory. At the time, it hardly seemed to matter; de Soto was sick with fever and, after reprimanding the officers, he withdrew into his tent.

The army knew that its general was dying. The fetid air of the Mississippi was conducive to fevers, and de Soto may well have caught malaria. Whatever the reason for his illness, the conquistador scarcely resisted its ravages. He seems almost to have welcomed it. His secretary was called to draw up his will, using a compressed cipher because of a shortage of paper. On the third day of the fever, the priests were summoned, and de Soto reconciled himself to death. His last act was to assemble his officers by his bedside and ask them to choose a new leader, but so great was their respect for the dying man that they asked de Soto to appoint his own successor. To their surprise he selected his disgraced lieutenant, the easygoing Luis de Moscoso. The next day, according to the chronicler, "departed from this life the magnanimous, the intrepid, the virtuous Captain, Don Hernando de Soto."

De Soto's death posed an immediate and macabre problem for the new commander. The Indians had believed that the white general was a demigod: the aborigine chiefs often claimed to be divine, and the invincible de Soto had fitted neatly into the same pattern. Moscoso was worried that if the Indians discovered that de Soto had died an ordinary death, they would lose their awe of the Spanish and launch an attack on the camp. To avoid this danger, de Soto's corpse was stealthily buried in the loose soil at the main entrance to the Spanish camp, where his grave

Somewhere in the huge area that they called Florida, de Soto and his men precariously negotiate one more river.

would be obliterated by the constant trampling of men and horses. However, this stratagem did not deceive the Indians, who quickly noticed the freshly turned earth and began asking pointed questions about the absence of the general. Fearing that the natives might dig up and perhaps mutilate the corpse, Moscoso had de Soto's body disinterred by night and carried down to the river. There it was wrapped in a shroud, weighted with sand, and dumped from a dugout canoe into the middle of the Mississippi. It was a strange burial ground for a Knight of Santiago who had set aside ample funds for a marble tomb in the church vault at Jerez de los Caballeros.

At first thought, Moscoso, the man responsible for the success of the disastrous Chickasaw fire attack, seemed an odd choice for the position of leader. But Moscoso had an even temper and was popular with both men and officers. He had joined the expedition in order to recoup his squandered Peruvian fortune, and when he saw that the new venture would not make a profit he had consistently advocated returning home. Furthermore, he had shown an uncanny instinct for survival, having weathered shipwreck, disgrace, defeat, and illness. By choosing Moscoso as his successor, de Soto made sure that the Florida expedition would eventually head for home.

Since the Indians were still curious about de Soto's whereabouts, they were told that the great general had ascended into the sky to consult his Father, and would be returning shortly. This was a lame excuse, and it was obvious that if the Spanish lingered they would be attacked once more. Moscoso knew that he had three alternatives: he could cross the Mississippi and return eastward the way the army had come, risking the vengeance of the tribes de Soto had antagonized; he could build boats, descend the river to the Gulf, and then sail westward along the Gulf coast to New Spain; or he could try to reach Mexico overland. Typically, he asked for the opinions of his officers. None of them wanted to try the long, hard march back to Tampa. They were equally frightened of the river trip, remembering that the Narváez expedition had drowned while attempting to flee the country in homemade boats. Therefore, they chose to try to march overland to Mexico. To forestall recriminations, Moscoso drew up an agreement and had all his officers sign it.

But the overland trek soon proved futile. As soon as the Spaniards passed out of fertile, well-populated regions into the desert country, they found themselves facing starvation. The army of Florida turned about and retraced its steps. In early December, the Spanish arrived on the banks of the Mississippi for the third and last time—no longer so much the army of Florida as the army of the Mississippi. They found two small, prosperous riverside towns, well stocked with provisions, and settled down in them to spend the winter building boats. The ingenuity of the Spanish troops was remarkable. Moscoso and his hidalgos knew that their lives depended on building these boats, and even the most aristocratic officers lent a hand.

The annual March rise of the Mississippi took them all by surprise and nearly ruined their painstaking efforts. And no sooner had they cleared away the debris than they had to deal with yet another Indian attack. (It was to be preceded, as in the Chickasaw country, by incendiaries, but this time the wary Moscoso took pains to learn the Indians' plans, and thwarted them completely.) At last, on July 2, 1543, the voyagers set out. There were 322 Spaniards, 100 of the healthiest Indian slaves, seven leaky pinnaces, 22 horses on rafts, and a flotilla of dugouts. They left behind about five hundred Indian prisoners, servants, and porters whom they had acquired on their travels. Most of these unlucky natives were far from their tribal homes, and the majority undoubtedly perished.

The first part of the journey was a nightmare of Indian harassment and foundering boats and rafts. The horses proved too difficult to transport and had to be killed or abandoned. But after a few days the pursuing natives finally gave up the chase and retired upstream. Then Moscoso and his men travelled alone down the Father of Waters for seventeen more days under a blazing sun. At last, on July 16, after seven hundred miles of river travel, they came within sight of the sea. Moscoso ordered the army ashore, and the soldiers repaired the boats for a sea voyage, filled the water kegs, and recouped their strength. But they dared not linger, because the delta Indians had learned of their presence.

On Wednesday, July 18, the expedition got under way for Mexico. For two days they rowed in the fresh water that the Mississippi poured into the Gulf, and then the flotilla stood out to sea and hoisted sails. The Spanish were lucky; the weather remained calm and the little boats, gunwales barely above the water, crept westward from headland to headland, their occupants suffering miserably from thirst and mosquitoes.

Finally, on September 10, fifty-two days after leaving the mouth of the Mississippi, they reached the Spanish settlement at the mouth of the Panuco River. Of the original 622 members of the Florida army, exactly half had returned to civilization. Like living scarecrows the survivors limped ashore and sank to the ground to kiss the sand and give thanks to God for their unforeseen salvation. But the credit for their survival belonged to their own incredible resilience and to Moscoso. The easygoing man of pleasure had extricated his force almost without loss from the heart of the continent. Using excellent judgment, he had succeeded where the more dashing de Soto had failed. It was his reward that he was the only man to make a profit from the venture—he wooed and married a rich Mexican widow and took her back to Spain, where, presumably, he lived the life of ease he had always craved.

Of the other survivors there is little record. A few stayed in the Americas to farm or join other conquistador armies; some made their way back to Spain; and one or two took holy orders in thanks for their deliverance. Nothing was ever heard of the Spanish deserters who had chosen to go native; the North American continent swallowed them without trace.

In the years that followed, Spain's colonial ambitions paid little attention to the "Rio Grande." There may have been some passing thoughts of an expedition tracing the river to its source in the interior, but de Soto's experiences had convinced the Spaniards that their efforts would be wasted. The Mississippi was not a highway to Golconda. A few trading posts were established near the delta but they did not prosper; the Spaniards turned increasingly to the problem of linking their older colonies rather than striking out into unknown territory, and it was not for another 150 years that white men sailed the Mississippi again. When they did, Spain was declining as a colonial power and the newcomers were Frenchmen arriving from the opposite end of the continent, the far northeast.

To write the book from which this article is taken, Timothy Severin, a young English historian, toured the length of the Mississippi. His book, Explorers of the Mississippi, *will be published by Alfred A. Knopf. In a forthcoming issue,* AMERICAN HERITAGE *will present the story of another, later exploration of the great river from Mr. Severin's history.*

As President of the United States, Ulysses S. Grant was not nearly so good at picking assistants as he had been when he was a general: his Cabinet, with few exceptions, was far from illustrious. Among Grant's worst appointments was George S. Boutwell, Secretary of the Treasury. He came to office at a time—1869—when the nation badly needed reforms in currency, taxation, and tariff policies; but "the one idea that flowered in his Sahara mind," historian Allan Nevins remarks, "was the reduction of the national debt."

One way to reduce the national debt, Boutwell figured, was to cut down on expenses and waste, starting with his own department. He took a tour through the Treasury Building, and announced that he had discovered the source of a serious leak in United States funds: there were too many female clerks employed by the Treasury Department, and most of them were not earning their keep. These excess persons, he decreed, would have to go—forthwith. And go they did.

While this move was regarded with consternation by the nation's feminists, to whom it was a serious setback in the struggle to improve the lot of the working girl, it struck the weekly magazines as quite amusing. Most of them were inclined to think, anyway, that woman's place was in the home, preferably a home where a number of weeklies were delivered regularly. Our pictorial display on these two pages shows how two of the weeklies—*Harper's Bazar* and *The Day's Doings*—reacted to Mr. Boutwell's economy measure. The *Bazar's* satirical engraving represents the moment when, supposedly, the new Secretary comes through the door into a room full of lady clerks who are engaged in such nonfiscal pursuits as decorating hats, playing practical jokes, using the ledger books as building blocks, and studying the latest fashions (in the *Bazar*, of course). One of them, who has moved on from folly to vice, is smoking a cigarette.

The Day's Doings provides the sequel: the departure of the clerks after the Secretary has issued his stern command. It is an interesting insight into the journalism of the period that whereas in *Harper's Bazar* the girls all appear to be rather elegant young ladies, in *The Day's Doings*—a salty New York publication that

A Low Blow for

the Working Girl

usually specialized in sex and crime stories—they look like trollops. One of the magazine's reporters wrote an accompanying story in the sharp style to which his readers had become accustomed:

The female element of the Treasury Department, at Washington, has come to grief, for a number of the fair employees of that department have received their congé. Fate is inexorable, and the hearts of our great officials are hard as stone. If tears could have melted them, if expostulations could have any effect upon them, if talk could have changed their purposes, if the light that lies in woman's eyes could have pierced into the official darkness of their souls, not a female Treasury clerk would ever have been dismissed, for it may readily be imagined that none of these were spared in behalf of the now placeless placewomen. But the fiat had gone forth, and there were none to save them; congressmen were invoked, even the President himself was importuned, but a just economy and the public weal overwhelm all personal or individual considerations; and so the Treasury girls departed, not as did the children of Israel from the land of Egypt among the walled-up waters of the Red Sea, but "more in sorrow than in anger" amidst the lamentations of their friends and would-have-been protectors [congressmen], who stood about the steps of the Treasury Building, as their fair ones, each with her little luggage, stepped forth from the gloomy pile which was to contain their beauties and witness their labors no more forever. Some of the dismissed dear ones left majestically, others wended their way mournfully, while not a few forgot their troubles in their native coquetry.

It was, indeed, a touching spectacle for the male congressional heart; and the male congressional heart, in consequence, throbbed convulsively, and the male congressional eye was suffused in unofficial tears. . . .

The male congressional eye might as well have remained dry. Behind the marching legions of feminism the female clerks have returned to the Treasury Department not in hundreds but in thousands, while George S. Boutwell has been profoundly forgotten. These days, though, if any of them are idle on the job, it's probably less a matter of goldbricking—Franklin D. Roosevelt put an end to *that* in 1933—than one of the doubtful benefits of the Computer Era.   —*E. M. H.*

ford. The terms required the colonists to pay him twopence per bushel for "all graine that shall be exported out of this River for ten yeares ensueing," sixpence per hundredweight for "Biskett," and twenty shillings for each hogshead of beaver. Later, the terms were changed to a flat payment of 180 pounds annually, one third in good wheat, one third in peas, and one third in rye or barley. After Lady Fenwick's death in 1645 George Fenwick returned to England. But Lion Gardiner bought an island off the tip of Long Island, named it after himself, and thus established a manor which has remained in the Gardiner family to this day.

The deal between Fenwick and the General Court at Hartford was typical of the barter system which the Yankees used from the beginning along the river highway and, in time, refined to the highest degree. The first building erected at the confluence of the Farmington and Connecticut rivers, at Windsor in 1633, was the Plymouth trading house, which in prefabricated form had been transported over water by William Holmes from Plymouth, Massachusetts.

William Pynchon, at Springfield, Massachusetts, was the first Englishman to establish a thriving river trade; because of the rapids at Enfield he built, in 1636, a warehouse just above Windsor, where he could unload his shallops and pinnaces and move the goods overland to Springfield or transfer the cargo to flatboats poled by a dozen stout men who, their labors eased by ample consumption of West Indian kill-devil, braved the rapids and reached Springfield by water. Pynchon's trade with the Indians was mostly in pelts, which he shipped to Boston. In fact beaver skins were such a common medium of exchange that when merchants struck the first coins or tokens, long before the issuance of government currency, that specie bore a crude image of the valuable little animal and the coins were popularly called beavers.

It was not long before Indian maize, tobacco, and other crops were being exported, not only to Massachusetts but after 1650 to England and the West Indies. Sailing masters found that the voyage upriver was in many ways more hazardous and certainly more frustrating than the ocean passage to the Indies. It usually took as long to sail from Saybrook to Wethersfield, two weeks, as to reach the mouth of the river from the land of rum and sugar. There was no dependable channel, there were no markers, no cuts through the sand bars—and no sailing was allowed on the Sabbath; they had to contend against strong tidal currents and fickle southwest winds impeded by the

hills. To beat to windward in such a narrow body of water was nigh impossible. Frequently, a vessel had to be towed by the crew, who carried a line ashore or who "walked" the ship by kedging an anchor upstream. Captain Lord of Glastonbury, in his sloop *Speedwell*, took twenty-six days to cover the ten miles from Glastonbury to Rocky Hill and wrote in his journal: "We can neither warp, tow, nor sail, and I feare me we never schalle." Next to the big bar at Saybrook, which had only six feet of water over it, the greatest obstacle in the seventeenth century was the double oxbow bend at Wethersfield, with its 180 degree turns, which forced river captains to anchor below Hartford for days and weeks at a time—and, incidentally, made Wethersfield the leading port of the period. Nature solved this problem in 1698, when a spring flood almost straightened the course of the river.

The colonists' dependence upon the river as the main artery of trade and travel for two centuries stimulated the growth of a prosperous shipbuilding industry. The first ship was launched at Wethersfield in 1649. She was the *Tryall*, built by Thomas Deming, whose yard was to keep busy until the middle of the nineteenth century. By 1700 small shipyards from Saybrook to Windsor were turning out vessels up to 100 tons. They started by copying the chunky, high-pooped English design, but soon turned to building the distinctive river sloops with their sharply raked masts and long bowsprits set at a sharp angle. Sometimes they were rigged with a square topsail and topgallant and carried an enormous square foresail to run before the wind.

Although seaworthy, the river sloops were hard to handle. Even so, often sailed by only a man and a boy, and with livestock on deck, they made regular trips to the Caribbean, where they cruised from island to

A view near Springfield, Massachusetts, about 1839

island, bartering Connecticut produce. They then returned to river wharves, where they became floating stores. Advertising their wares in the *Courant*, the owners offered to exchange them for salt pork, wheat, lumber, tobacco, onions, horses, and cloth, which they carried south on their next voyage. Rum was by far their leading import, and tippling was so prevalent that an early almanac contained this ditty:

> *Ill husbands now in taverns sit*
> *And spend more money than they git.*
> *Calling for drink, and drinking greedy*
> *Tho many of them poor and needy—*

While their sloops were venturing to distant horizons, the colonists had to find ways of crossing the river itself in order to carry on their daily tasks. There was no bridge until 1808. Cable-operated ferries quickly appeared. The first was Bissell's at Windsor in 1648; it was operated by the family for three generations. For a while the Hartford ferry used a horse on a treadmill —enclosed in a cage to prevent contact with passengers —which turned a paddlewheel amidships. On a 1794 map of the state six ferries appear; as many as fifteen existed from time to time, including private ones like that of gunmaker Sam Colt (the largest employer on the river), which transported employees from the Colt armory across to East Hartford. (There are still two ferries in operation.) The Chester-to-Hadlyme ferry was originally a sailboat belonging to a man named Warner, who presented it to his son as a wedding present with the stipulation that if he earned more than thirty dollars a year in tolls, the excess must be returned to his father. When a traveller wished to cross there, he blew on a tin horn attached to a large maple tree near the landing.

By the middle of the eighteenth century shipbuilding on the river had reached its peak, and it continued to prosper almost without interruption for another hundred years, despite two wars and the introduction of competing forms of transportation. Over seventy vessels, locally built and owned, and employing nearly 500 men in their crews, were in service in the mid-seventeen-hundreds. Haddam had "nine great shippes" on her ways at one time, Essex thirty. At this time the sloops were giving way to larger craft like the new schooners and brigs. An English officer visiting Hartford in 1764 wrote in his journal: "Here they build vessels, for the Lumber Trade to the West Indies, from 100 to 150 tons, and float them down in Freshes, in Spring and Fall." When the Revolution came, the town of Essex gave the colonies their first homemade warship, the 24-gun *Oliver Cromwell*, built by Uriah Hayden. Her twelve-foot draft made her the largest craft to cross the Saybrook bar, and before being captured by the British three years later she succeeded in taking nine prizes. In the course of the war, the Connecticut navy comprised thirteen vessels, in addition to nearly three hundred commissioned privateers. The river itself was defended by the fort at Old Saybrook, with a battery of six guns and a twenty-man garrison.

After the victory of the colonies, river commerce revived. The increasingly larger and heavier ships plying the Connecticut forced merchants to do something about the main obstacle to more profitable cargoes—the lack of a dependable channel from Hartford to the mouth. In 1773 the first real move to improve navigation had been made by the assembly when, goaded by the Hartford merchant Jeremiah Wadsworth, it had voted to raise money by lottery for marking the Saybrook bar. Still, the average depth was less than six feet. In 1784 one of Wadsworth's captains advised him that he had brought a load of salt to New London and there engaged two small craft to carry about a thousand bushels to Hartford, and he hoped this action would "lighten ship so she will go over Saybrook Bar with a common Tide." Even at high tide loaded sloops and schooners could not reach Hartford under sail. At great expense and delay it was often necessary to warp them across the sand bars or unload their cargoes into lighters below Middletown. As a result of Wadsworth's petition to the legislature, the Union Company was chartered in 1800 to deepen the river bed below Hartford, to construct wharves, and to collect tolls to pay for the improvements.

The War of 1812, highly unpopular in New England, brought about a coastal blockade and caused the Connecticut River merchants severe hardships. During the conflict English men-of-war boldly invaded the river, set fire to Essex, and burned twenty-three ships. To reduce their risks, the Hartford merchants entered into partnerships, taking shares in various vessels and adventures. There was even joint underwriting of ship insurance, at 5½ or 6 per cent interest, with individual liability commonly limited to 100 pounds. These experiences were an important factor in making Hartford a world insurance capital.

The river merchants were the center of the power structure of this period; they made up what Vernon Parrington called "a small, interlocking directorate [that] controlled religion, business, and politics." Staunch Federalists, good Congregationalists, they were the bulwark of a social system that did not change until the Industrial Revolution. Their fortunes, based in most instances on smaller ships, were not as impressive as those of the great Massachusetts shipping moguls with their ocean ports; but in proportion to the total population of the colony there were more shipping fortunes. Called the "river gods," these shipowners and merchants supplied the American armies of several wars, helping to make Connecticut famous as the arsenal of the nation.

A new era arrived suddenly for the Connecticut in 1815, when the steamboat *Fulton* churned upriver between the scows and sloops cluttering the channel and docked in Hartford for thousands to see. Rigged as a sloop, in case sails were needed—as indeed they often were—she made a dreadful din with her wood-fired engine, which gave off sharp, staccato blasts of steam. The *Courant* enthused: "Indeed it is hardly possible to conceive that anything of its Kind can exceed her, in elegance and convenience." She was designed by Robert Fulton, the man popularly acknowledged to be the inventor of the steamboat, despite the fact that John Fitch, a native of Windsor who died by his own hand in penury, had successfully used steam to propel vessels seventeen years before Fulton. "The day will come," Fitch had prophesied, "when some more powerful man will get fame and riches from my invention; but nobody will believe that poor John Fitch can do anything worthy of attention."

Four years after the *Fulton*'s debut a steamboat was launched at Hartford and functioned as a towboat along the river. There quickly followed regular steamboat service thrice weekly on the *Enterprize* of Captain James Pitkin, who advertised that passengers could be landed "at any place on the river at their pleasure." The *Oliver Ellsworth*, in 1824, was the first of a long line of "floating palaces" that cruised the river in the next half century. Built by the Connecticut Steam Boat Company, she was 112 feet long, 24 feet in beam, had an eight-foot draft, and weighed nearly 230 tons. Her 44-horsepower engine enabled her to average eight knots. Sleeping 62 persons and carrying 400 passengers, at five dollars apiece, she made three trips a week between Hartford and New York, the approximately 140-mile voyage sometimes taking as little as eighteen hours. This same year, "amidst the salute of cannon and the shouts of thousands of gratified and grateful spectators," the aged Marquis de Lafayette left Hartford aboard her during his last, triumphal visit to America.

Travel on the early side-wheelers, with their crude cross-head engines and undependable copper boilers, was at best a hazardous undertaking. Three years later, when in the sound about four miles from Saybrook light at seven thirty in the evening, the *Oliver Ellsworth*'s boiler exploded, and the steam injured several persons and killed a fireman. She managed to sail into Saybrook, whence an excited postrider galloped to Hartford, burst in upon the legislature sitting in the old statehouse, and shouted: "The Eliver Ollsworth . . .

biled her buster!" Not long after, the *New England* blew up at Essex, killing or maiming fifteen out of seventy people aboard. Despite these disasters, the number of steamboats on the river increased sharply after 1840. River traffic, although the railroad whistle was already sounding its death knell, was then at its peak, and three competing steamboat lines served New York. In 1846 there were over 2,000 arrivals and departures of sail and steam vessels at Hartford's twenty-odd wharves, even though the town's population was barely 13,000.

In the 1820's the Enfield rapids limited traffic above Hartford to flatboats carrying less than ten tons, and Hartford's merchants were frustrated by their inability to make the fullest use of the river for trade northward with Massachusetts, New Hampshire, and Vermont. Further, their business was threatened by the granting of a charter, in 1822, to a New Haven group to build the Farmington Canal, paralleling the river route. The ditch, which was actually built (and is now a weed-grown freight railroad track), headed north, bypassing all the river ports some miles to the west, and finally joined the Connecticut at Northampton, Massachusetts. In 1824 the Hartford interests formed the Connecticut River Company and obtained a charter for the purpose of improving upstream navigation above Hartford. Eager to demonstrate that the river was far superior to the canal for economical transportation, they at once decided to prove it with a steamboat. In mid-November of 1826 a stern-wheeler called the *Barnet,* only seventy-five feet long and drawing less than two feet, arrived at Hartford, having been towed from New York. She was to cause a tremendous sensation. It was reported that one man followed her some distance along the shore and exulted that the boat went just as fast as he could walk. Fearing the river would soon freeze, her owners wasted no time. Leaving Hartford November 17, she reached Warehouse Point, site of Pynchon's warehouse, where the larger scows still unloaded their cargoes; her first

George Fenwick, an early settler, built this monument at Saybrook for his young wife, who died there in 1645.

102

attempt to climb the rapids failed. Two days later, with a scow lashed to each side and manned by thirty fallsmen with poles, she succeeded, and at Springfield "twice 24 guns announced and welcomed her arrival...." At every stop during the two-week trip she was met with cheers and the firing of cannon. Most of the country folk had never seen a steamboat before. At Bellows Falls, Vermont—the northern terminus of her trip—a banquet was tendered the crew and effusive toasts were drunk: "Connecticut River—Destined yet to be the patroness of enterprise, and to bear upon her bosom the golden fleece of industry," and "The grand highway from Canada to the seaboard. Give us steam!" Her backers were ecstatic. For the first time a steamboat had ascended 200 miles above the tidewaters of the river at the marvelous speed of six miles per hour against current and head wind.

Thus encouraged, the merchants proceeded with the building of the Enfield canal, a six-mile-long, seventy-foot-wide ditch to get around those rapids, deep enough to accommodate large flatboats and steamboats up to seventy-five tons. (In 1795, with the construction of the canal at South Hadley, Massachusetts, to bypass the Hadley Falls, the Connecticut had become the first river in the United States to be so improved.) Four hundred Irishmen arrived as workmen, their worldly goods tied in red bandannas, and in 1829 the Enfield canal opened to traffic. Fifteen boats passed through the first day, including Thomas Blanchard's new stern-wheeler *Vermont*. Soon stern-wheelers were chugging daily between Hartford and Springfield, going up through the canal and down over the rapids. Tolls were one dollar per passenger and fifty cents per ton of freight. In February of 1842, Charles Dickens made a downstream trip in the *Massachusetts*, which he described as having "about half a pony power." Actually, it was nearly twenty. In his *American Notes*, he wrote:

Fortunately, however, the winter having been unusually mild, the Connecticut River was "open," or, in other words, not frozen. The captain of a small steamboat was going to make his first trip for the season that day (the second February trip, I believe, within the memory of man).... Mr. Paap, the celebrated Dwarf, might have lived and died happily in the cabin, which was filled with common sash-windows like an ordinary dwelling-house.... But even in this chamber there was a rocking-chair. It would be impossible to get on anywhere, in America, without a rocking-chair.... I may state that we all kept the middle of the deck, lest the boat should unexpectedly tip over.... The river was full of floating blocks of ice, which were constantly crunching and cracking under us; and the depth of water ... did not exceed a few inches.... The Connecticut River is a fine stream; and the banks in summer-time are, I have no doubt, beautiful....

Dickens was less enamored of the leading citizens of Hartford whom he met upon arrival: "Too much of the old Puritan spirit exists in these parts to the present hour; but its influence has not tended, that I know, to make the people less hard in their bargains, or more equal in their dealings."

Two years after his voyage the completion of the railroad between Hartford and Springfield signalled the eventual end of the boom days for both the upper river and the steamboats which used it. But the Enfield canal still had its uses; it was converted to a source of power for the paper and textile companies springing up along the river. Even today its four locks are operable, and powerboats go through them to return to the mouth of the Connecticut at the start of each yachting season. On the lower river, between Hartford and the sound, however, travel only increased.

In the years before the Civil War river steamers were transporting more than ordinary passengers and goods. With abolitionist sentiment strong in New England, many a shipowner, like Jesse G. Baldwin of Middletown, Connecticut, found room on his vessel for runaway slaves and thereby made the river a link in the underground railroad. Steamboats bringing southern cotton to Connecticut mills not infrequently carried fugitives, and Old Lyme was an active underground railroad center. In Hartford the most prominent abolitionist was Francis Gillette, a United States senator and father of the famous actor William Gillette. At his Nook Farm, which later became the focus of the city's intellectual life and where Charles Dudley Warner, Harriet Beecher Stowe, Joseph Hawley, and Mark Twain were to live, Gillette gave food and shelter to dark-skinned travellers who came and went in secrecy. The slave trade never played a significant role in Connecticut's economy. In 1784 the legislature had provided for gradual emancipation of the 6,500 slaves then in the state; by 1830, there were only 23 slaves left out of a Negro population of some 8,000, and in 1848 the legislature abolished slavery.

After the Civil War, thanks to the excellent steamboat service, the river developed into a popular resort area for the carriage trade of New York City. The Haddams in particular attracted summer visitors. At East Haddam was Goodspeed's Hotel, one of the many enterprises of an unusual Yankee fireball by the name of William Goodspeed, who was, besides being a hotelkeeper, a successful shipbuilder, merchant, and banker. To capture and hold the tourists arriving by steamboat at his hotel, he conceived the idea of an opera house ornately decorated in the manner of a steamer saloon. Finished in 1877, Goodspeed's Opera House was an instant success. Entire shows were brought from Broadway, often for a one-night stand. Josh Billings,

Bloodgood's Minstrels, and orators of note, such as Henry Ward Beecher, all played Goodspeed's. The large drop curtain depicted the steamer *State of New York*—the last and most elegant of the side-wheelers—passing below East Haddam. Ironically, in 1881 the *State of New York* struck a hidden snag and was beached with a big hole in her bottom at almost the identical spot shown on the curtain. A promoter at heart, Goodspeed was more than equal to the occasion. He raced to the balcony of the Opera House which overlooked the river and instructed the captain of the ferryboat *Goodspeed* to bring the 150 passengers to see the show at his expense and to spend the night at his hotel. It is said that the next day he offered a twin bill: *Uncle Tom's Cabin* at the Opera House and a visit to the wrecked steamer. Her wreck forced the Hartford & New York Steamboat Company into receivership, and from then on, in diminishing numbers and elegance, the steamboat continued to fight a losing battle against the railroad and the highway, until the *Hartford* made its last trip during the early 1930's. Goodspeed's Opera House has recently been beautifully restored, and operates as a theatre, but the great passenger steamers whistle up no more.

The first half of the twentieth century on the Connecticut, as on many American rivers, was memorable mainly for a series of disastrous floods. In November, 1927, a great flood swept down the Connecticut Valley from Vermont, killing some twenty-one people and causing a property loss estimated at fifteen million dollars. Another terrible flood hit the valley in March of 1936, when eleven lives were lost and more than thirty-five million dollars in property was destroyed. This finally led to a public outcry for flood-control dams on the tributaries of the Connecticut, and many of these have now been constructed. The hurricane of 1938 struck the valley particularly hard. New England had not had a hurricane since 1815, and advance warnings were few. The river rose, covering highways and railroads, and the high winds denuded the towns of the valley of most of their trees.

Today, beneath the fine new skyline at Hartford and through a maze of superhighways, the river runs almost forgotten. Here no docks remain, only a few old pilings and bulkheads that give mute testimony to what used to be, and the dikes shut out any view of the stream itself. Worse than man's neglect of the river has been his abuse of it, especially of this upper section, where the tide is almost imperceptible, and where no cleansing salt water sweeps in from ocean and sound. The Connecticut has earned the unsavory reputation of being dirty, smelly, and unfit for man, fish, or bird. Concern over the river's condition was expressed as early as 1884 by J. B. Olcott of South Manchester, who wrote: "A land with its rivers running filth instead of pure water, is like a body with its veins running filth instead of pure blood . . . Hartford sits nervously in the lap of what was once one of the fairest and sweetest, and is now one of the filthiest valleys in the world." Nevertheless the Connecticut is still vital to agriculture, industry, and power. Along its banks Yankee farmers produce thirty million dollars' worth of shade-grown and broadleaf cigar tobacco annually, while factories use millions of gallons of the river daily for cooling and processing.

Surprisingly, the old Valley Railroad still serves river industry also; twice a week it runs from Middletown to Essex though the bed of the single track has become so bumpy that the maximum speed limit has been cut to twenty miles per hour. But the panorama from the diesel cab of the little freight train, as it rumbles along close to the river, is breathtaking. Below a feldspar quarry and a power station is a lonely stretch of woodland and hills that seems to have changed little since Block sailed by. The train cuts its way through the branches and brush on either side, occasionally scaring a partridge or rabbit, whistles by the deserted private crossings, and passes summer cottages facing the river, marinas, and boat-launching ramps. At the stops there are none to greet the train, there is no bustle of activity, only a car or two to drop off or pick up. The ride seems to lead one right back into the past.

More essential to Connecticut industry than the railroad is the river highway itself, and the tugboats, barges, and tankers that ply it year round, carrying three million tons of cargo upriver annually, more than half of it oil. The U.S. Army Corps of Engineers maintains a fifteen-foot channel from Old Saybrook to Hartford, and the Coast Guard sees to it that over 100 navigation lights are kept in working order, including—since 1839—the sentinel guarding the mouth. In winter, the Coast Guard also keeps the channel open, using 100-foot tugs that can easily slice through two feet of ice.

With tens of thousands of pleasure craft now registered, and boating recognized as the Number One family sport, the river is fast becoming a great and noisy recreation highway. Numerous public launching sites, yacht clubs, marinas, small shipyards, and state parks dot the lower river, mostly below Middletown, where the water is saltier and a little cleaner. Army engineers are debating opening up the Connecticut above Hartford by dredging a channel for small boats all the way to Holyoke. At the same time, the water resources of the entire basin are being studied by the federal government to consider its recreational future and the possibility of preserving it as a unique kind of national park. Thus, despite the pollution and other changes, in many ways the river is being used for the sports and pleasures of yesteryear. Over 100,000 shad a year are still caught in the Connecticut, college crews race at Hartford, and diesel excursion boats cruise daily in good weather between Hartford and Middletown or give sightseers a peek at the lotus lilies of Selden's Creek just above Brockway's Landing and at the bygone splendor of the Haddams, where the picturesque castle of William Gillette sits atop the hill known as the Seventh Sister. Gliding past, one can almost hear again the cry of the bosun on the steamboat creeping upriver, calling out the landings: "Hadlyme, Haddam, North Haddam, East Haddam, Middle Haddam, Wish the devil had 'em!"

Between Essex and the entrance the marshes remain a naturalist's paradise, even though the onslaught of civilization has reduced them to two thirds of their former size. Here, on land washed twice a day by salty tides, muskrats scamper through waist-high grasses and bulrushes; sandpipers poke about in search of insects; and wild duck and heron and osprey make their seasonal visits. Slip down in a sailboat past the marshes, the little towns, and the neat lighthouses, and you are in Long Island Sound, still pulsing with the same currents that carried in Adriaen Block over three and a half centuries ago. What vast changes all that time has seen!

Ellsworth S. Grant, a Hartford businessman and a descendant of Thomas Hooker, is vice chairman of the Connecticut governor's Clean Water Task Force. He sails the river and in the summer lives at its very mouth, at Fenwick.

Firebrand of the Revolution CONTINUED FROM PAGE 64

to the King might be touched by the royal hand, he growled that it would more likely be spurned by the royal foot.

In November, 1772, Sam managed to set up a Boston Committee of Correspondence to link the Massachusetts towns. Within a few months other towns had followed suit, and he had a taut organization poised to act at his command. A discerning Tory declared it the "foulest, subtlest, and most venomous serpent ever issued from the egg of sedition."

In fact, everything Sam did for a decade smacked of sedition. As early as 1768 Hutchinson had secretly sent depositions to England to see if there might be grounds for his arrest. Parliament dusted off a neglected statute of Henry VIII that would bring all treasonable cases to London for trial. Tories were sure that Sam would now end on the gibbet, where he belonged. They gloated that he "shuddered at the sight of hemp." A Londoner wrote jubilantly to Hutchinson: "The talk is strong of bringing them over and trying them by impeachment. Do you write me word of their being seized, and I will send you an account of their being hanged." But the British solicitor general took a long look at the evidence and decided that it was not sufficient—yet.

Meanwhile Sam was out to ruin Hutchinson, and didn't care how he did it. To beat the devil any stick would do. The chance came in 1772 when Ben Franklin, then in London as an agent for the Massachusetts House, laid hands on a bundle of letters written by Hutchinson and Andrew Oliver to correspondents in England. Franklin sent them to Boston with instruc-

tions to share them among the trusted inner circle of patriots and return them uncopied and unpublished. Whether he meant these instructions to be strictly obeyed, or issued them for his self-protection, we do not know. The patriots brooded over the letters for several months; then Sam announced that "a most shocking scene would soon open," and that a vicious plot against American liberties would be disclosed.

Expectation of horrifying news was raised to a fever pitch. In June, 1773, Sam ordered the House galleries cleared. He told the members in grave tones that he had letters vital to their concern, but that they must first swear neither to copy them nor make them public. At this Hancock rose to say that someone unknown to him had thrust copies of letters into his hand on the street. Might they be the same as those held by Mr. Adams? If so, were the letters not already abroad? Yes, to be sure, they were the same; obviously they were abroad. The House decided that the letters should no longer be concealed.

Hutchinson's correspondence was really fairly mild, and said little that he had not already stated openly, but Sam managed to put it in the worst possible light. When the letters were published, passages had been slyly snipped from their context, and an outraged commentary had been so mixed with the text that the unwary reader was easily led to see an evil purpose when none was intended. Other letters in the packet were more damaging than Hutchinson's, but he was neatly smeared with their brush. He suffered great discredit even in the rural villages, where most of his conservative support lay. The House petitioned the

King, asking that Hutchinson be removed from office.

Now the storm was gathering. Alone of the revenue acts, the duty on tea remained. For years Boston matrons had boycotted the rich English brew, and instead had concocted somewhat unsavory beverages of catnip and mint. Prompted by the desperate straits of the East India Company, Parliament tried in 1773 to help the company unload its embarrassing stockpile of tea on the colonies. Boston patriots decided that the flesh should not be so tempted. While ships bearing 342 chests of tea lay at the wharfs, Sam gave the signal and a band of his mechanics disguised as Mohawk Indians whooped off toward the harbor. As every schoolboy knows, they dumped the whole cargo into Massachusetts Bay. "Sam Adams is in his glory," said Hutchinson; and he was.

Parliament retaliated in a rage. In March, 1774, it ordered the port of Boston clamped shut. It decreed that after August 1 the Provincial Council, which formerly had been elected by the House, would be named by the governor, as would the higher judges. The royal sheriff would select all juries; town meetings throughout the province would assemble only with the governor's consent, and discuss only what he authorized. General Thomas Gage, commander in chief of His Majesty's forces in America, supplanted Hutchinson as governor. By June, four regiments of redcoats were encamped on the Common. This was the showdown; it was knuckle under or risk war.

Sam knew that to pit Boston (population 17,000) against British power was to place the mouse beneath the lion's paw. "I wish we could arouse the continent," he had written to a fellow patriot the year before. Now, in the spring of 1774, the continent was awakening: a Continental Congress was in the making. How could this matter be discussed and delegates elected before Gage got wind of it and prorogued the Massachusetts legislature? He already had moved the House temporarily from troublesome Boston to the Tory stronghold of Salem; the town swarmed with redcoats.

For ten days the House dispatched routine business with disarming amiability while Sam lined up votes behind the scenes. On June 17, when all was ready, he suddenly ordered the doors of the meeting hall locked. Sensing a plot, one Tory member slipped past the doorkeeper and hurried away to alert Gage. Sam put the key in his pocket and presented a slate of delegates (of which he was one) to attend the Congress, set for Philadelphia in September. Gage scratched off a hurried order to dissolve the House, but the messenger beat on the door in vain. Inside, the House leisurely elected the delegates and assessed the towns for their expenses.

For the first time in his life Sam Adams was to leave

Sam Adams' patriots seemed to get a great deal of aggressive satisfaction from beating up stamp-collectors in effigy.

the shores of Massachusetts Bay. He still lived in the crumbling ancestral home on Purchase Street, with land running down to the harbor, where he had a small dock. The household consisted of his second wife, Elizabeth Wells Adams (his first wife had died in 1757), a son and a daughter by his earlier marriage, a servant girl, and a shaggy dog famed for biting redcoats. Elizabeth Adams was devoted and above all frugal, for since their marriage his only earnings had been the meager allowance granted him as clerk of the House of Representatives. Fortunately he had few personal wants, and would live on bread and milk and dress in threadbare clothes, if the cause of liberty were thereby served. "He says he never looked forward in his Life," recorded Cousin John, with Yankee amazement at such carelessness, "never planned, laid a scheme, or formed a design of laying up any Thing for himself or others after him."

Friends put together the money to outfit him for the journey to Philadelphia. He was resplendent in new suit, wig, hose, shoes, and cocked hat; he swung a gold-topped cane, and in his pocket there was a much-needed purse of money. On August 10, 1774, the delegation—John Adams, Sam Adams, Thomas Cushing, and Robert Treat Paine—rolled out of Boston in full array—coach, coachmen, and mounted servants.

They were received with great honor along the route, but friendly patriots in Philadelphia advised them that the other colonies were suspicious of Boston's hot-headed radicals. John Adams summed up their warning: "You must not utter the word independence, nor give the least hint or insinuation of the idea, either in Congress, or any private conversation; if you do, you are undone, for independence is as unpopular in all the Middle and South as the Stamp Act itself. No man dares speak of it...."

During the seven-week session the Massachusetts delegation stayed discreetly in the background. When Sam urged that an Anglican clergyman be permitted to open the sessions with prayer, southerners decided that the dour Calvinist might have some good in him after all. But he was bold in opposing any concessions to Britain: "I should advise persisting in our struggle for liberty, though it was revealed from heaven that nine hundred and ninety-nine should perish, and only one of a thousand survive and retain his liberty. One such freeman must possess more virtue and enjoy more happiness than a thousand slaves; and let him propagate his like, and transmit to them what he hath so nobly preserved."

From 1774 to 1781 Sam Adams' public life was bound up with successive Congresses. He brought to them the same stubborn energy and forehandedness that had worked so well in Boston. "He was constantly holding caucuses of distinguished men," Jefferson recalled, "... at which the generality of the measures pursued were previously determined on, and at which the parts were assigned to the different actors who afterwards appeared in them." His name bobs up almost daily in the congressional journal. Joseph Galloway, leader of the conciliatory wing in the Congress, recognized him as one to keep a wary eye on, "a man who, though by no means remarkable for brilliant abilities, yet is equal to most men in popular intrigue and the management of a faction. He eats little, drinks little, sleeps little, thinks much, and is most decisive and indefatigable in the pursuit of his objects. It was this man, who, by his superior application, managed at once the faction in Congress at Philadelphia and the factions in New England."

Sam was ready for independence when most Congress members still clung to compromise. Philadelphia Quakers were for leaving the issue to Providence; he tartly replied that Providence had already decided for liberty. To James Warren in Plymouth he wrote during the spring of 1776: "The Child Independence is now struggling for Birth. I trust that in a short time it will be brought forth, and, in Spite of Pharaoh, all America will hail the dignified Stranger."

In July he signed the Declaration of Independence, and with that stroke of the pen signed away his real vocation. Success put him out of business. America no longer needed an agitator; now it had to defeat an army in the field and build a new nation.

Sam admitted that he was unfit for "founding Empires," and in various ways he proved it. In Congress he favored a citizen militia until forced to concede that the war could be fought only with a more permanent army and a unified command. Frankly critical of Washington's Fabian tactics, Sam was widely accused of involvement in a cabal to replace him, but there is no evidence to support the charge. He disapproved of any social gaiety in so grave an hour, and had Congress pass rules forbidding members to attend balls or entertainments. They voted the rules, and diligently ignored them. His weakness for government by committee led the French minister to lament over the man "whose obstinate, resolute character was so useful to the Revolution at its origin, but who shows himself so ill-suited to the conduct of affairs in an organized government."

Yet Sam worked with his old doggedness through the dark years of war. Jefferson considered him "more than any other member, the *fountain* of our more important measures." At the low ebb of American fortunes in October, 1777, he was one of only twenty members who stuck with Congress. "Though the smallest," Sam remarked, "it was the truest Congress we ever had." He was on the committee that framed the Articles of Confederation in 1777. Four years later, when Congress celebrated their ratification with a keg of wine and some biscuits, Sam alone remained of the original drafters. In April, 1781, he went home and never crossed the borders of Massachusetts again.

He returned, like Ulysses, to find his hall full of strangers—the young, the new postwar merchants: unfamiliar faces, other times. John Hancock, who had been elected first governor of independent Massachusetts, led Boston a merry romp of feasts and revels; it was far from the "Christian Sparta" of which Sam still dreamed. The old radical was elected to the state Senate and became its president, but he was no longer invincible. In 1783 and again in 1787 he lost the race for the rather empty and unsalaried office of lieutenant governor; in 1788 a youngster defeated him for the first Congress under the federal Constitution. But in 1789, when he teamed with Hancock to become lieutenant governor, some enthusiasts wrote his name on their ballots in gold. At Hancock's death in 1793 he succeeded to the governor's chair, and was re-elected by solid majorities for three more one-year terms.

Changing times even forced the revolutionary into the camp of reaction. As president of the Senate, which under the state constitution required its members to have an estate of four hundred pounds, he headed a body designed to check the democratic excesses of the House. Some Bostonians thought the town's growth warranted a change to representative government; Sam reported for his committee that the town-meeting system had no defects in it. Debtors in the western counties who in 1786, under a Revolutionary War veteran named Daniel Shays, resorted to mob violence discovered in the former rebel an implacable foe. He branded them "banditti" and urged the execution of their leaders. Popular opinion was more merciful; Hancock commuted the death penalty. As governor, Sam vetoed a bill to permit stage performances, and

Bostonians howled that he was robbing them of their natural rights. Toward the dispossessed Tories, others softened, but Sam's hatred burned with its old fierceness. He would not have a British subject left on American soil nor, indeed, admitted by naturalization.

But Sam had not really changed at all, and that was his misfortune. He earned the lasting enmity of Federalists by his opposition to the new federal Constitution proposed in 1787. Shocked to discover that it would set up "a National Government instead of a Federal Union of Sovereign States," he declared himself "open & decided" against it. But he also insisted that the state convention called in 1788 to ratify the federal Constitution give the document the careful paragraph-by-paragraph discussion that it deserved. Antifederalists who wanted a quick vote while their hostile majority was intact pleaded financial inability to stay for a long session. Sam dryly remarked that if they were so pressed he would dig up funds for their living expenses.

Very likely some of the fight went out of him with the death of his doctor-son while the convention was going on. According to one story, the Federalists finally swung him around by a shrewd move. They staged a meeting of Sam's beloved mechanics at the Green Dragon Inn, where resolutions were passed urging ratification. Daniel Webster wrote a dramatized account of how Paul Revere brought Sam the news:

" 'How many mechanics,' said Mr. Adams, 'were at the Green Dragon when the resolutions were passed?'

" 'More, sir,' was the reply, 'than the Green Dragon could hold.'

" 'And where were the rest, Mr. Revere?'

" 'In the streets, sir.'

" 'And how many were in the streets?'

" 'More, sir, than there are stars in the sky.' "

Sam, Webster tells us, thought that over a while. To him, the voice of the common man was as close to the voice of God as one could get. "Well," he mused, "if they must have it, they must have it."

He retired from public life in 1797, and lived six years more in a yellow frame house on Winter Street. Its parlor was hung with engravings of the great champions of liberty. He liked to sit on the doorstep or wander in the little garden, talking about old times. Death came on October 2, 1803, when he was 81 years of age.

The Federalist regime in Massachusetts was embarrassed about full burial honors for its political foe. The governor was absent; no subordinate dared risk a misstep, and the first suggestion was a modest cortege of school children. Aroused at this, friends rallied a fitting processional of state and town officials, dressed out with a muster of cadets. But eulogies delivered in the Massachusetts House were whittled down for public consumption. In Congress no member from Sam's state rose to memorialize him. It fell to Virginia's John Randolph of Roanoke to remind the House that a great patriot had died. With these small honors "The Father of the Revolution" went to his last sleep in the soil of a free and independent America.

Alexander Winston specializes in Revolutionary and pre-Revolutionary history. Currently, he is working on a book about three famous seventeenth-century pirates: William Dampier, Henry Morgan, and William Kidd.

For further reading: Samuel Adams, by James K. Hosmer (Houghton, Mifflin, 1898); Sam Adams, Pioneer in Propaganda, by John C. Miller (Little, Brown, 1936).

Goggles & Side Curtains

CONTINUED FROM PAGE 38

turn, and look out for the cars!" The last was a reference to the sobering fact that in those days there were hardly any railroad over- or underpasses.

As the utility poles became decorated with more and more insignia—sometimes there were as many as eleven represented on one pole—the situation became chaotic. Detours were still poorly marked, and feeder roads caused confusion since they carried the same markings as the main route. Finally, there were not enough color combinations to serve the needs of The O.K. Short Line, the Blue Grass, the Cannonball, and all the rest.

In many parts of the West there were no poles to paint. In 1914 one traveller reported finding the information he needed crudely daubed on a five-gallon gasoline can beside the road. In Colorado an auto tourist discovered his directions painted on the bleached skull of a buffalo. An inquirer at Albuquerque, New Mexico, who was headed for Los Angeles, received these instructions: "Follow the mountain range eighty miles south to a stick in the fork of the road with a paper tied to the top. Take the ruts that lead off to the right."

The big confusion over road markings was removed by a simple expedient. Roads began to be designated by numbers instead of colored rings of paint. In 1917 a beginning was made when Wisconsin adopted the numbering system in use today. Minnesota followed in 1920, and the plan was adopted in 1925 by the United States government for routes of interstate and national significance, the even numbers running east and west, the odd numbers north and south. Thus the famous red, white, and blue rectangles of the Lincoln Highway faded away as that celebrated route, along with all the other "trails," lost its identity to the numbered U.S. metal shields that tied the new system together.

Yet many important roads were still unsurfaced. Looking back at the situation that prevailed when the numbered routes were adopted, an official in the Wisconsin State Highway Department has offered these words of consolation: "You knew you were on the right road even though you were stuck in the mud."

The motorist's faithful assistant in shaping his itinerary was one or another of the automobile "tour books." These guides had been issued since the early years of the century by motor clubs, advertisers, or established publishers such as Rand McNally & Co., most of whom were already sophisticated in the techniques of mapping. An *Official Automobile Blue Book* ("There's one in nearly every car") was distributed by the American Automobile Association from the middle of the first decade until the twenties. A compilation of road information between important points like Rochester, New York, and Buffalo, the *Blue Book* was perhaps the most famous and widely used specimen of this genre of touring literature, which traced its ancestry back to the modest bicycle map.

A trip into unfamiliar territory required homework. The adventurer studied his manual, debated the choice of routes, weighed data on road surfaces, and noted prominent landmarks. He knew that mechanics were scarce: if the machine broke down, the only resource might well be a village blacksmith who could, hopefully, weld a broken spring or solder a leaky radiator, but who would scarcely be up to penetrating the mysteries of a balky carburetor float. The driver expected to patch his own tires and pump them up with his own hand pump. Gasoline could be looked for at a general store, drug store, or dry-cleaning establishment. It was drawn from a wooden barrel out back somewhere and was poured through a funnel from a one-gallon measure. Windshields were not wiped. Air was not free. The only rest room was the bushes.

With tour book in hand and odometer set at zero, the tourist started out on an itinerary usually measured in the manual from a prominent spot like the courthouse, the post office, or a leading hotel. The operator of the car required the services of a companion who could keep one eye on the mileage figures and landmarks noted in the "motorlogue," the other checking the printed information against the readings on the odometer. A third eye would often have been helpful. If the navigator missed the white church on the right,

He: "Is the tire flat?"
She: "Well, it's a little flat at the bottom, but the rest of it is all right."

while the driver was busy with the clutch or the spark, trouble was sure to overtake the party when the *Blue Book* and the odometer failed to agree.

Suppose, for illustration, one wished in 1915 to travel by motor from Norwich, Connecticut ("The Rose of New England"), to Willimantic. Starting from in front of the Wauregan Hotel, with odometer adjusted to 0.0 miles, the machine chugged up the long, terraced hill of Broadway. The surface was "good macadam" and one progressed in this manner:

01.8 fork; left by green—end; left
04.0 YANTIC, mill, fork; right—by sta
07.7 fork; bear right thru hills
09.7 N. FRANKLIN, fork; turn right
13.1 S. WINDHAM, sta; left—trolley; right
16.0 fork; right under rr—end; left
16.5 WILLIMANTIC, sta; go W, MAIN ST.

In addition to providing itineraries, the motor logs also offered interesting background information likely to advance the cause of tourism. For instance, one could read in a tour book sponsored by the Mohawk Rubber Company that Elkhart, Indiana, was the home of the celebrated Dr. Miles's patent-medicine almanac, issued annually in editions of 12,000,000, and that "52 per cent of band instruments of the world [were] made here. . . ." Of Spotsylvania, Virginia, a tour book said: "Solomon's Store; gas," and added this historical footnote: "Around here in May, 1864, Grant opposed Lee in a series of the bloodiest battles of the Civil War. Many homes still have cannon balls lodged in the walls."

Sometimes touring was complicated by poor local directions, the ultimate being the advice of the confused countryman who lives on in automobile folklore for having declared, "You can't get there from here." A well-known phenomenon was the Auto Hater. Farm houses displayed hostile signs—"No Water." Between Buffalo and Cleveland, the *Blue Book* gave this direction in 1909: "At 11.6 mi., yellow house and barn on rt. Turn left." But there was no yellow house. The owner had uncharitably repainted his premises green because, as a neighbor explained to an inquirer, "He's agin' automobiles." Scattered tacks and broken glass strewn at prominent intersections were also tried by the antiauto faction as a means of holding back the swelling motor tide.

The difficulty of handling a bulky book in an open car moving at cruising speed led to the invention of ingenious attachments designed to reveal the correct route mechanically. Both these expensive accessories and the ubiquitous logbooks were superseded by the handy, folded road map. It went far beyond charting just the heavily travelled routes between fixed points —Chicago and South Bend, Los Angeles and Santa Barbara. The numbering system made it possible for the road maps to identify *all* the roads. And a notable feature of the new maps was—they were free.

The give-away maps were introduced by a new facility, the "filling station," which delivered measured quantities of gasoline from curbside pumps. There is a dispute as to who built the first real filling station and where. Semantics are involved. What constituted a real filling station? The new kind of gasoline merchant appeared almost simultaneously in various regions where competition was keen. Primitive filling stations are reported as existing in St. Louis, Dallas, and Seattle in 1907. Detroit's first was a crude shed at First and Fort streets, knocked together in 1910 from some old voting booths. Among its customers was Henry Ford. The shape of the future may be discerned in a station built in Memphis in 1912 by the Standard Oil Company of Louisiana. It had thirteen pumps, a ladies' room, a maid who served ice water.

Many early filling stations, now more often called service stations, looked rather like cracker boxes. With success, however, their architecture grew fanciful, to harmonize with the neighboring real-estate developments; in southern California, mission-style structures were favored. Elsewhere the motorist drove up to pagodas, sea shells, castles, or lighthouses, with illuminated globes on top of the pumps beaming out the brand name of the gasoline sold there.

The man who thought up the free road map was William B. Akin, head of a Pittsburgh advertising agency. Akin was himself an enthusiastic automobilist who knew how it felt to get lost on nameless roads. The whole concept came to Akin while he was driving his 1912 Chalmers along Baum Boulevard. He took the suggestion to the Gulf Oil Company in the fall of 1913. His proposal was that the company prepare, publish, and distribute a map of Allegheny County, Pennsylvania, as an advertising scheme, with copies to be

 # Travel Hints for Early Motorists

Use chewing gum to mend a leaky gas line.

Carry a can of ether for winter starting.

Test for an overheated engine: Spit on it. If there is a sizzle, all is well. If steam rises, check your radiator.

Strain all gas through a chamois skin to remove water and dirt.

If the spark lever slips while you are cranking, tie it in position with a piece of string.

A box of oatmeal flakes is handy when the radiator springs a leak. Pour flakes into the water. As they swell they fill the hole. Dried horse manure is also good and, of course, always available.

To rejuvenate a worn tire, pump in a cupful of chopped-up feathers and hot molasses. Spin tire to distribute the mixture evenly and seal pores and holes. Watch out, though, if there is a blowout.

A gun is no longer needed when you visit the western states.

To clean the Celluloid windows in your side curtains, use vinegar.

To keep windshield clear on rainy days, rub sliced onion over it.   —G. C.

mailed to all registered car owners in the area and handed out at the company's new drive-in filling station, another Gulf innovation. The thing was done. It was an instant hit. State maps followed in 1914.

"Gulf was quite cute about all this," an old-time employee recalled. "We used this map . . . to persuade the customer to come back for another map for another trip. Hence, not too much territory or information was included in any one map."

But the whole industry, by the early twenties, was producing easy reference maps in enormous quantities. Oil companies were to the American road what Baedeker was to Europe. While the automobile population exploded, the maps, along with the gas pumps and the courteous men who hand-cranked them, became indigenous to the travel scene. No longer did Dad have to be a spiritual descendant of Henry the Navigator to dream of driving west from the Oranges in New Jersey to spend the winter at Pasadena. One question did remain to be answered: What about food and lodging on the way?

As the inn had developed in response to animal-drawn transportation and the modern hotel had followed the spread of the railroad network, a new social entity known as the "auto tourist camp" came into being. Almost unknown in 1918, well-established by

1923, the camps were located in a field or woodland where motorists pitched their own tents and prepared their own meals. Some camps were free, operated perhaps by a retail dealer who sold oil, gas, and a few groceries. "Camping at garage," one tour book noted of Fairview, Pennsylvania, in 1923. But the movement was toward modestly priced "pay" camps. Some were located in city parks and provided water, a cookhouse, common dining hall, sanitary facilities, and police protection—all for about fifty cents a day. On the road between Dodge City, Kansas, and Lamar, Colorado, the U-Smile Auto Camp, a privately run place, offered similar facilities for twenty-five cents a day. But whatever the price range, the mood among the auto gypsies was one of fun and release from life's tedium. Their social atmosphere was more egalitarian than in most areas of American life. Conversations were easily started; one glanced casually at the license tags on a dusty auto and found it natural to inquire, "What part of Iowa are you folks from?"

Just stay two nights at the Santa Barbara auto park, the saying ran, and you would be asked to a party, especially if you could play the violin, read palms, or turn the crank on the ice cream freezer. These holiday-makers constituted a new leisure class who were seeing America's natural wonders through goggles and side curtains while enjoying the exhilaration of swift movement and new contacts. Theirs was a quest of the spirit, too, as they shared enchanted evenings at the band concert in the park, the fragrance of the summer night around them, and the stars swinging above.

There was a rapid upgrading of facilities, including the innovation of tourist cabins. At Camp Grande, at El Paso, Texas, the gasoline tourists in 1925 found prices ranging from fifty cents to five dollars a day (for a "de luxe bungalette"). There was a central recreation hall furnished "about like a country club," and electric irons could be rented from the office. Denver's chief motor camp, called Overland Park, was a veritable metropolis of the thermos bottle and the khaki lean-to; it frequently checked in between five and six thousand open-air guests in one night. The camps expanded to meet the demand. The total of such stopping places for the whole country was estimated in 1925 at between four and five thousand.

But weary travellers tired of pitching tents, of breaking camp every morning, and of generally playing Indian. The preference shifted to a room of one's own, a real room in a real house. Private homes hung out a sign that became increasingly familiar, "Tourists Accommodated." Simultaneously, refinements were added to the "cabin" concept with the appearance of specially designed "cottage courts," which soon spread from the West to the East.

From there it was but a short step to the motel. As far as can be ascertained now, the term originated with a California architect, Arthur S. Heineman, who opened a motor court at San Luis Obispo in 1925 which he called "The Milestone Motor Hotel." Designed in the mission style, it consisted of a series of detached cabins arranged around a court behind a main building that housed the office. The first motel lacked, it is true, room TV, skeet shooting, saunas, a thirty-two-lane bowling alley, and an indoor swimming pool with fireplace. But the owner did provide a lounge and dining room. According to a possibly apocryphal story, Heineman couldn't get the full name of his hotel on his roadside sign, and coined the word "motel."

After World War I, when automobiles had acquired front and rear bumpers and passengers were enclosed in the protective all-steel sedan, the motorist expected as a matter of course to find at every service station free air, free water, free windshield and crankcase service, free comfort conveniences, and an old tire, painted white, advertising FLATS FIXED. On the road he could count upon such amenities as a dog wagon offering red hots, or a pretty tea house with screened porch, ruffled curtains, pottery glazed in apple green, and "Home-Cooked Meals." More and more tourists gladly exchanged cash for experience, and returned home, like all travellers from time immemorial, with strange tales of marvels seen and heard, and the insignia of high adventure pasted on the windshield—the red deer symbol of Mount Rainier or the green buffalo of Yellowstone Park. As Stephen Vincent Benét sang in his unfinished epic, *Western Star*, *"I think it must be something in the blood"*—and tourism made it a something remembered as land, clouds, history, sounds, smells, people. And, of course, as signs flashing smoothly by: KIWANIS CLUB MEETS EVERY TUESDAY, VISITORS WELCOME ... CLEAN REST ROOMS ... SEE THE HISTORIC SHRINE ... SMOKE BULL DURHAM ... HOT FRANKS AND GLADS ... DON'T MISS THE CAVERNS ... ANTIQUE SHOPPE ... WILD SAGE HONEY 100 YARDS AHEAD.

The Open Road was, at last, open.

A seasoned chronicler of American folkways, Gerald Carson is old enough to remember side curtains himself—dimly.

For further reading: Fill 'er Up, by Bellamy Partridge (McGraw-Hill, 1952); Wheels on the Road, by David Hebb (Collier Books, 1966).

"He'd Have to Get Under, Get Out and Get Under," by Maurice Abrahams, Edgar Leslie, and Grant Clarke. © 1913 Maurice Abrahams Music Co., Inc. Copyright renewal 1941 Robbins Music Corporation, Edgar Leslie and Fred Fisher Music Co., Inc. Used by permission.

Ambrose Bierce's Devilish Definitions

"Wit stabs, begs pardon—and turns the weapon in the wound," Ambrose Bierce once wrote, succinctly explaining his own, often black, type of humor. This American satirist originally wrote his Devil's Dictionary *in installments, as columns in various San Francisco magazines during the late nineteenth century. First brought together in book form in 1906, the sardonic lexicon has become an American classic. Only recently was it discovered that about half the definitions Bierce originally wrote have never been included in any edition of the book, presumably because he compiled the material, years after writing it, from incomplete files. Ernest J. Hopkins has now assembled the missing definitions, and Doubleday & Company will bring out later this month the first complete collection, to be called* The Enlarged Devil's Dictionary. AMERICAN HERITAGE, *impressed with the durability of Bierce's demonic wit, presents a sampling of the new material.*

Adam's apple, *n.* A protuberance in the throat of man, thoughtfully provided by Nature to keep the rope in place.

affectionate, *adj.* Addicted to being a nuisance. The most affectionate creature in the world is a wet dog.

ardor, *n.* The quality that distinguishes love without knowledge.

> He loved her with an ardor—
> Such a hot one,
> That her father had to guard her
> With a shotgun.—Ovid

bachelor, *n.* A man whom women are still sampling.

bequeath, *v.t.* To generously give to another that which can no longer be denied to *somebody*.

betrothed, *p.p.* The condition of a man and woman who, pleasing to one another and objectionable to their friends, are anxious to propitiate society by becoming unendurable to each other.

biography, *n.* The literary tribute that a little man pays to a big one.

Buddhism, *n.* A preposterous form of religious error perversely preferred by about three-fourths of the human race....

circumlocution, *n.* A literary trick whereby the writer who has nothing to say breaks it gently to the reader.

coquette, *n.* A vain, foolish and stupid girl who after a pretty thorough sampling of oneself prefers another.

coroner, *n.* (Latin, *corona*, a crown; the pronunciation "crowner" is therefore legitimate.) A municipal officer charged with the duty of cutting up the unfortunate to see if they are dead. They always are.

courtship, *n.* The timid sipping of two thirsty souls from a goblet which both can easily drain but neither replenish.

dandle, *v.t.* To set an unresisting child upon one's knee and jolt its teeth loose in a transport of affection. A grown girl may be similarly outraged, but her teeth being more firmly secure, there can be no object in doing so....

defendant, *n.* In law, an obliging person who devotes his time and character to preserving property for his lawyer.

dentist, *n.* A prestidigitator, who puts metal into your mouth and pulls coins out of your pocket.

deposit, *n.* A charitable contribution to the support of a bank.

depraved, *p.p.* The moral condition of a gentleman who holds the opposite opinion.

desertion, *n.* An aversion to fighting, as exhibited by abandoning an army or a wife.

deshabille, *n.* A reception costume for intimate friends varying according to locality, *e.g.*, in Borrioboola Gha, a streak of red and yellow paint across the thorax. In San Francisco, pearl ear-rings and a smile.

divorce, *n.* A resumption of diplomatic relations and rectification of boundaries.

fault, *n.* One of my offenses, as distinguished from one of yours, the latter being crimes.

forbidden, *p.p.* Invested with a new and irresistible charm.

governor, *n.* An aspirant to the United States Senate.

gratitude, *n.* A sentiment lying midway between a benefit received and a benefit expected.

haughty, *adj.* Proud and disdainful, like a waiter.

hedgehog, *n.* The cactus of the animal kingdom.

hireling, *n.* A mercenary wretch who serves another person for wages, as distinguished from the respectable functionary who receives a salary.

homesick, *adj.* Dead broke abroad.

hunger, *n.* A peculiar disease afflicting all classes of mankind and commonly treated by dieting. It is observed that those who live in fine houses have it the lightest. This information is useful to chronic sufferers.

reservation, *n.* A place where wicked Indians are taught the Christian virtues.